BRAIN BUILDERS!

500

MIND-BLOWING

S.T.E.M.

FACTS FOR KIDS!

FOR KIDS AGES 6-10 YEARS OLD!

TABLE OF
CONTENTS

THE
WORLD
OF
S.T.E.M.

E=mc²
2x2=4
S.T.E.M
SCIENCE • TECHNOLOGY • ENGINEERING • MATHEMATICS
H₂O
2x2=4
H₂O

THE WONDERFUL WORLD OF S.T.E.M.

Hey there, awesome explorers! Get ready to strap on your boots, grab your magnifying glasses, and dive headfirst into a treasure chest overflowing with the coolest, most mind-boggling facts ever. This isn't your everyday, snooze-fest fact book. Oh no! This is your ultra-mega, super-duper, fantastically fun guide to the whole wide world of STEM—Science, Technology, Engineering, and Mathematics. But lean in for the secret... it's all about unveiling the wonders and mysteries that make our world an extraordinary place to explore!

Imagine if you could talk to robots, or if you knew the secret handshake to make computers do backflips for you. What if you could build a fortress so strong, even a dinosaur couldn't knock it down? Or maybe you've wondered why dogs sniff everything, why ice cream melts (and how to stop it—because, let's face it, melted ice cream is a tragedy), or why the moon looks like it's following you home. Guess what? STEM is the key to unlocking all these mysteries and more!

First off, we're going to zoom through space like super-speedy astronauts. We'll dodge asteroids, surf on comet tails, and discover why planets don't just bump into each other. Ever thrown a ball and watched it curve? It's the same fancy footwork that keeps the planets twirling around the sun instead of flying off into the galaxy.

Next up, ever wondered what makes you, well, you? Why can your friend roll their tongue into a taco shape and you can't? It's all in the magic of biology! We'll dive into the mini-worlds inside us, from the jungles in our bellies (yes, there are creatures living there, and they're pretty friendly) to the superhighways of nerves zipping messages from your toes to your nose.

But wait, there's more! Have you ever mixed baking soda and vinegar and watched the fizz-tacular volcano eruption? That's chemistry, the secret recipe behind making pizzas and turning leaves into gold in the fall. It's like being a wizard, where mixing different potions can create something totally unexpected (but let's leave the explosions to the experts, okay?).

And then, we get to build stuff! Engineering is like playing with the world's biggest set of LEGOs, except these blocks can create robots, bridges, and even your favorite amusement park rides. We'll find out how engineers are like the superheroes of building, making sure everything stands tall, stays put, and doesn't get blown over by the big bad wolf.

Of course, we can't forget about technology. Thanks to tech, we can chat with friends on the other side of the planet, play video games with people we've never met, and take photos that make our breakfasts look like they belong in a museum. We'll explore how technology is like a magic carpet, ready to whisk us off to anywhere we can imagine.

As we journey deeper into the heart of STEM, we'll uncover the mysteries of how things work, why they work, and what makes them so incredibly awesome. We'll start with the smallest of the small – atoms, the tiny dots that make up everything from your favorite candy to the moon and stars. Ever wonder why some things float and others sink? Or why mixing certain things can cause an explosion of colors (or just a plain old explosion)? That's chemistry showing off, proving that even the tiniest particles can throw a massive party.

But hold on to your hats, because we're not just sticking to the Earth. We'll catapult ourselves into the realm of computer science, where ones and zeros create entire worlds, solve mysteries, and even do our homework (well, sort of). We'll crack secret codes, discover how video games are made, and maybe even meet a robot or two that can dance better than any human. It's like discovering a secret language that controls the world around us, from the phone in your hand to the car that drives you to school.

Now, take a deep breath, because we're also about to dive into environmental science, where you'll learn how to be a hero for our planet. Discover how trees talk to each other, why bees are so buzz-worthy, and what you can do to keep Earth smiling. It's like being part of an elite team of planet protectors, using science to save the day and make sure we all have a beautiful, clean home for generations to come.

And just when you think you've seen it all, we'll explore the electrifying world of physics, where forces, motion, and energy dance together in the grand ballet of the universe. Ever throw a paper airplane and watch it glide gracefully (or nosedive spectacularly)? That's physics in action, showing us the beauty of flight, the thrill of speed, and the power of pushing against the air itself.

But wait, there's a twist! Did you know that math is the secret sauce that makes all of STEM come together? It's the language of the universe, the rhythm of the stars, and the blueprint for everything from the pyramids to your local playground. We'll unlock the mysteries of numbers, patterns, and shapes, showing you that math isn't just about adding and subtracting; it's about discovering the secrets hidden in everything around us.

So, are you ready to laugh, learn, and leap into the unknown? Are you prepared to ask the big questions and chase down the answers? Then let's keep turning those pages, because every fact is a clue, every chapter a new world, and every discovery a victory in the grand adventure of STEM. Together, we'll unravel the wonders of the universe.

The journey is just getting started. With every experiment, every question, and every curious thought, you're not just learning—you're becoming a scientist, a technologist, an engineer, and a mathematician. You're becoming the future. And who knows? Maybe one day, you'll be the one creating books like this for the next generation of curious minds!

Chapter 1

THE WONDERS OF SPACE

1. **The Sun: The Solar System's Spotlight** - The Sun is like the biggest spotlight in our solar system, shining on every planet's performance. It's so huge, you could fit over a million Earths inside it!

2. **Mercury: The Speedy Messenger** - Mercury zips around the Sun faster than any other planet, like it's delivering space mail on super-speedy rollerblades. It's the solar system's speedster, completing a solar lap in just 88 days.

3. **Venus: The Cloudy Mystery** - Venus is shrouded in thick clouds, making it the solar system's master of disguise. You might think

it's playing hide and seek, but really, it's just
very shy about showing its surface.

4. **Earth: The Life Party** - Earth is the only
    place we know that's hosting a life party,
    with humans, animals, and plants on the guest
    list. It's like the universe's favorite hangout
    spot, complete with oceans for swimming and
    forests for exploring.

5. **Mars: The Red Desert** - Mars, the Red
    Planet, is like the desert of the solar system,
    but with giant volcanoes and valleys. It's
    famous for its red dirt, perfect for cosmic
    gardening if you don't mind wearing a space
    suit.

6. **Jupiter: The Giant With A Red Spot** - Jupiter
    is so big, you could fit all the other planets
    inside it and still have room for dessert. It's
    also got a giant storm called the Great Red
    Spot, which is like a never-ending tornado
    party that's been raging for centuries.

7. **Saturn: The Ringed Beauty** – Saturn wears a set of dazzling rings, making it the fashion icon of the solar system. It's like it decided to accessorize with billions of ice and rock particles because plain planets are just too mainstream.

8. **Uranus: The Sideways Roller** – Uranus rolls around the Sun on its side, like it decided to be different and do cartwheels through space instead of spinning. It's the solar system's rebel, showing off its unique style.

9. **Neptune: The Windy Wanderer** – Neptune is the windiest place in the solar system, with storms faster than the fastest racecars. It's like it's always in a hurry, hosting the most extreme weather events for any daring space explorers.

10. **Pluto: The Dwarf Planet** – Once considered the ninth planet, Pluto is now known as a dwarf planet. It's like the solar system's little sibling, still part of the family but playing by its own rules out in the Kuiper Belt.

11. **Asteroids: The Solar System's Leftovers -** The asteroid belt is like the solar system's leftover building materials, floating between Mars and Jupiter. It's as if the planets had a giant construction project and forgot to clean up after themselves.

12. **Comets: The Cosmic Snowballs** - Comets are like dirty snowballs flying through space, lighting up when they get close to the Sun. They're the universe's way of throwing a spectacular light show across the sky, with long, glowing tails.

13. **The Milky Way: Our Galactic Home** - The Milky Way is our sprawling galactic home, filled with billions of stars, including our Sun. It's like living in the biggest, most star-studded city in the universe, with a view that's out of this world.

14. **Black Holes: The Cosmic Vacuum Cleaners** - Black holes are like the universe's vacuum cleaners, sucking in anything that gets too close. They're the mystery spots of space

where even light can't escape, perfect for
cosmic hide-and-seek, but you might not want
to find them!

15. **Shooting Stars: Wishes in Motion** - Shooting
stars are not stars at all but meteoroids
burning up in Earth's atmosphere. They're
like nature's fireworks, zipping across the sky
so you can make a wish, no birthday cake
needed.

16. **Alien Worlds: The Universe's Exotic
Destinations** - Exoplanets, or planets around
other stars, are like the exotic vacation spots
of the universe. Some might have oceans,
others could have endless rain of glass—truly
the ultimate adventure spots, if only we could
get there!

17. **The Northern Lights: Earth's Light Show**
- The Northern and Southern Lights are
like Earth throwing its own light parties in
the sky, with solar particles dancing in the
atmosphere. It's the planet's way of saying,
"Let's light up the night!"

18. **Space Exploration: Humanity's Greatest Adventure** - Space exploration is like humanity's biggest, most daring adventure, reaching for the stars and discovering the universe's secrets. It's our real-life science fiction, proving the sky's not the limit, after all.

19. **The International Space Station: Our Home in the Sky** - The International Space Station is like a high-tech treehouse orbiting Earth, where astronauts live, work, and occasionally play with their food in zero gravity. It's the ultimate science lab, zooming around the planet at 17,500 miles per hour.

20. **Galaxies Beyond Our Own: The Cosmic Web** - Galaxies are like cities in the vast country of the universe, with the Milky Way being just one of billions. Imagine each galaxy as a bustling metropolis where stars, planets, and black holes live, work, and play in their cosmic neighborhoods. It's like space has its own version of an intergalactic Google Maps, but with way more twinkling lights.

21. **The Zodiac: Space's Storybook** - The Zodiac constellations are like the universe's own storybook, with each group of stars telling a different tale from ancient myths. It's as if the night sky is a giant picture book, and the constellations are illustrations that have been used for thousands of years to tell stories about heroes, monsters, and epic adventures.

22. **Auroras on Other Planets: Extraterrestrial Light Shows** - Just like Earth, other planets in our solar system have their own versions of the Northern and Southern Lights. Imagine Jupiter throwing a light show party that's even bigger and more colorful than Earth's, with auroras so bright you could read a book by them—if you could stand on Jupiter without turning into a space pancake, that is.

23. **The Oort Cloud: The Solar System's Icy Shell** - The Oort Cloud is like a giant, icy shell surrounding our solar system, filled with comets that occasionally visit us. It's as if the solar system lives in its own snow globe, and every now and then, a snowflake breaks free and zooms towards the Sun for a fiery show!

24. **Meteor Showers: The Universe's Firework Display** - Meteor showers happen when Earth passes through trails of cosmic debris, lighting up our atmosphere with streaks of light. It's the universe's way of throwing a firework display, with no two shows ever quite the same. It's like space is saying, "Check this out!" with a spectacular light show just for us.

25. **Space Stations and Satellites: Humanity's Eyes and Ears in Space** - Space stations and satellites orbit Earth like tiny moons, watching over us and sending back information. They're like the planet's collection of high-tech gadgets, spying on weather patterns, mapping the land, and even streaming TV shows. It's as if Earth has its own set of smart devices, all floating around above us.

26. **The Phases of the Moon: The Lunar Light Show** - The Moon changes shape from night to night, from a thin crescent to a full glowing orb and back again. It's like the Moon has its own set of moods, showing off different personalities throughout the month.

It's Earth's natural nightlight, with a dimmer switch controlled by the universe.

27. **Solar Eclipses: The Cosmic Dance** - A solar eclipse happens when the Moon passes between the Sun and Earth, casting a shadow over us. It's like the Sun, Moon, and Earth are all lining up to take the perfect cosmic selfie. For a moment, day turns to night, and we get a sneak peek at the universe's behind-the-scenes magic.

28. **Space Rovers: The Robotic Explorers** - Space rovers are like remote-controlled cars, but instead of racing down the driveway, they're trekking across alien worlds. They're humanity's robotic explorers, sent to places like Mars to take pictures, collect rocks, and even sing "Happy Birthday" to themselves. It's like having a space-faring pet that sends you postcards from the Red Planet.

29. **Zero Gravity: The Floating Fun Zone** - In space, there's no up or down, and astronauts float as if by magic. It's like being in a

pool where you don't have to swim, and
you can eat floating blobs of water and
do somersaults in the air. It's the ultimate
playground, where the rules of gravity don't
apply, and every jump is a giant leap.

30. **The Speed of Light: The Universe's Speed
Limit** - Light travels at an unimaginably fast
speed, zipping through space so quickly that
it can go around the Earth 7.5 times in just
one second. It's like the universe set a speed
limit, and light is the cosmic racecar driver
that always obeys the rules. If you could ride
a beam of light, you'd be the fastest traveler
in the galaxy, but you'd never get a speeding
ticket!

31. **The Big Bang: The Universe's Birthday
Party** - The Big Bang theory explains how
the universe started with a giant explosion,
expanding and cooling to become everything
we see today. It's like the universe's own
birthday party, where instead of balloons
and cake, there were stars and galaxies as
party favors. And it's still going on, with the
universe getting a little bigger each year.

32. **Alien Life: The Universe's Mystery Guests** -
The search for alien life is like the universe's
biggest game of hide and seek. Scientists use
telescopes and space probes to peek under
cosmic rocks and behind gas clouds, hoping to
find the universe's mystery guests. Whether
they're tiny microbes on Mars or intelligent
beings sending signals from faraway stars,
we're eager to meet the neighbors.

33. **The Habitability of Planets: The Cosmic Real
Estate** - Finding planets that could support
life is like scouting for the best cosmic real
estate. Scientists look for "Goldilocks" planets,
not too hot, not too cold, but just right for
life as we know it. It's as if we're browsing
the universe's housing listings, looking for the
perfect spot with just the right conditions
for our next vacation home.

34. **Star Formation: The Cosmic Nursery** - Stars
are born in vast clouds of gas and dust,
collapsing under gravity until they're hot and
dense enough to shine. It's like the universe
has its own nurseries, where little baby
stars bundle up in their dusty blankets until

they're ready to light up and join the galaxy's twinkling population.

35. **Asteroid Impacts: The Cosmic Messengers** - Sometimes, asteroids visit Earth a little too closely, leaving behind craters as cosmic calling cards. It's like space is playing a game of interstellar bowling, and occasionally, a stray ball ends up in our lane. These space rocks tell us stories of the solar system's past, like reading an old diary filled with tales of cosmic adventures (and a few close calls).

36. **Gravity: The Invisible String** - Gravity is the invisible force that keeps us grounded and makes planets orbit stars. It's like the universe has invisible strings attached to everything, pulling apples down from trees and keeping the Moon circling around Earth. Without gravity, we'd all be floating around, which might sound fun until you try to drink water or play soccer!

37. **The Life Cycle of Stars: Cosmic Beginnings and Endings** - Stars, like people, go through

life stages: they're born, they live, and they
eventually die, sometimes with a spectacular
bang as a supernova. It's as if the stars
are putting on their own life drama in the
sky, with some choosing to exit the stage
in a blaze of glory, leaving behind beautiful
nebulae or dense black holes as mementos.

38. **The Color of Stars: A Stellar Rainbow** –
The color of a star tells us how hot it is,
from cool red stars to hot blue ones. It's
like stars choose their outfit based on their
temperature, with each one sporting a
different color to show off its heat. Next time
you look at the night sky, remember you're
gazing at a cosmic rainbow of starry styles.

39. **The Voyager Probes: Humanity's Message
in a Bottle** – The Voyager probes are like
cosmic message bottles we've thrown into the
sea of space, carrying greetings and music
from Earth. They're on a mission to tell any
alien finders about us, kind of like sending
a postcard that says, "Greetings from Earth!
Wish you were here (or maybe just wish you
knew we were here)."

40. **Dark Matter: The Universe's Mystery Ingredient** - Dark matter is the stuff we can't see but know is there because it affects how galaxies spin. It's like the universe's secret recipe ingredient, making things work even though we're not quite sure what it is. Imagine trying to bake a cake with an invisible flour that you know is super important but doesn't show up no matter how much you squint.

41. **The Kuiper Belt: The Solar System's Attic -** The Kuiper Belt is a region beyond Neptune filled with icy objects, like a storage attic for the solar system's leftover bits and pieces. It's where Pluto and its friends hang out, reminding us that even at the edge of our solar neighborhood, there are still treasures (and maybe some old holiday decorations) to discover.

42. **The Aurora on Jupiter: The Giant's Light Show** - Jupiter has its own version of the Northern and Southern Lights, created by its strong magnetic field. It's like the gas giant decided not to miss out on Earth's light show

parties and threw its own spectacular bash, complete with the biggest, most colorful lights in the solar system.

43. **Exoplanet Atmospheres: Peeking into Alien Skies** - Scientists can now peek into the atmospheres of planets around other stars, looking for clues about their weather and maybe even signs of life. It's like spying on your cosmic neighbors to see what color they painted their skies and if they have clouds that look like puppies, just like we do.

44. **The Speed of the Solar System: Earth's Galactic Road Trip** - Our whole solar system is zooming through the Milky Way galaxy at an astonishing speed. It's like Earth and all its planetary friends are on a road trip across the galaxy, but without the need for snack stops or bathroom breaks. Buckle up; we're all in for a long ride!

45. **Supernovae: The Universe's Fireworks** - When a star explodes as a supernova, it outshines entire galaxies for a brief

moment. It's the universe's way of setting off fireworks, celebrating the end of a star's life with a spectacular light show that astronomers can see from billions of miles away.

46. **Interstellar Travel: Dreaming of Cosmic Journeys** - The idea of traveling to other stars captures our imagination, even though it's currently beyond our reach. It's like dreaming of the ultimate vacation to exotic, far-off worlds, where the locals might have tentacles instead of toes and where the souvenirs are truly out of this world.

47. **Saturn's Moons: A Family of Oddballs -** Saturn's family of moons includes some of the strangest characters in the solar system, from Titan with its methane lakes to Enceladus shooting water into space. It's like Saturn is the parent of a very diverse and slightly wild cosmic family, each with its own peculiar hobbies.

48. **The Solar Wind: The Sun's Breath** - The solar wind is a stream of charged particles blown out by the Sun, creating space weather that can affect Earth. It's as if the Sun is exhaling, and its breath travels all the way to our planet, sometimes creating beautiful auroras, the Earth's way of blushing.

49. **Cosmic Rays: The Universe's Tiny Messengers** - Cosmic rays are high-energy particles that travel across space, bombarding our atmosphere. They're like tiny, invisible messengers from distant parts of the universe, delivering notes that scientists are eager to read. It's the universe's way of sending us postcards, written in a language we're still learning to understand.

50. **The Moon: Earth's Night Light** - The Moon is Earth's loyal companion, the biggest and brightest object lighting up our night sky. It's like a trusty night light that never needs batteries, perfect for lighting up epic nighttime adventures in your backyard.

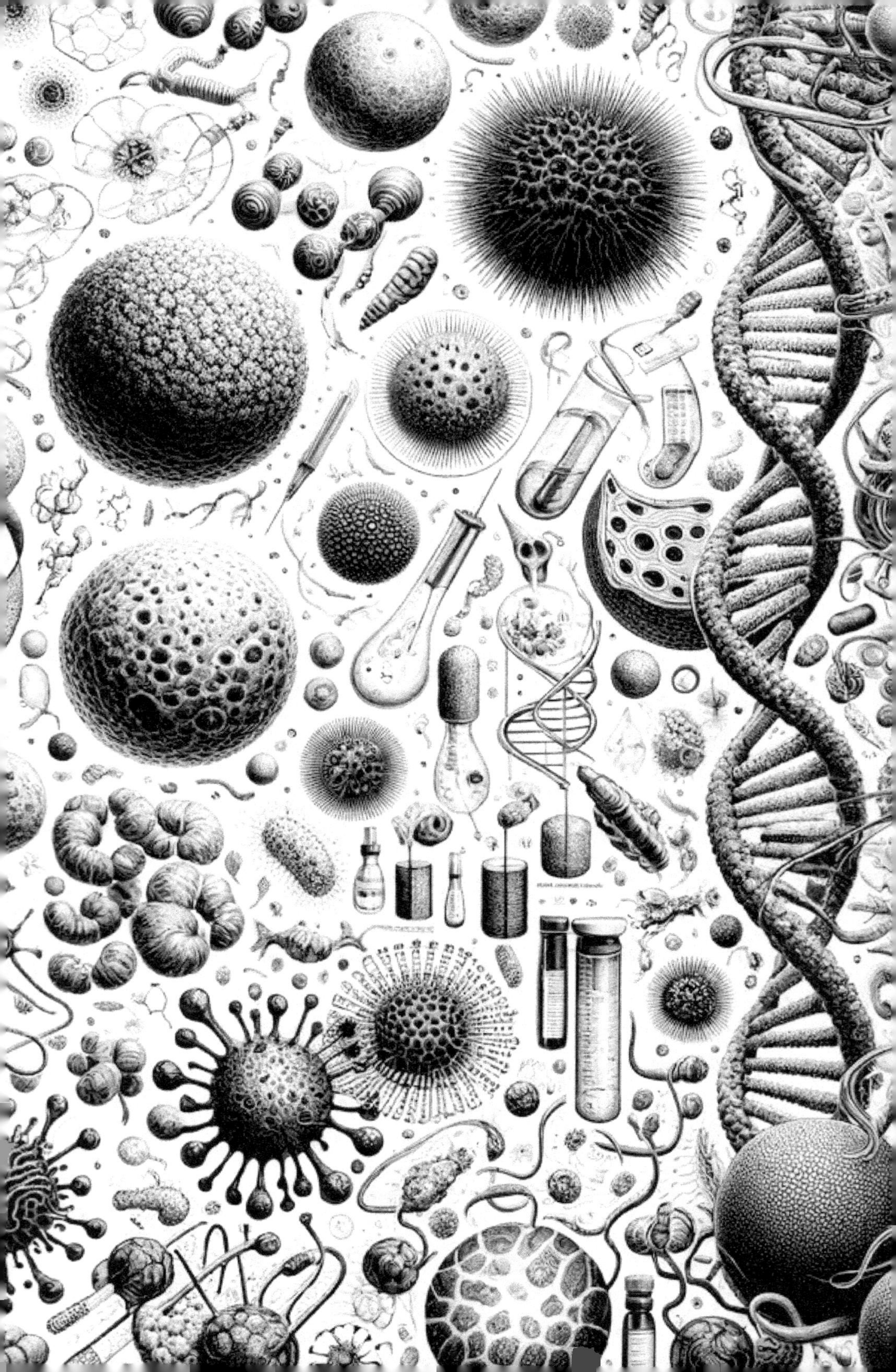

Chapter 2

THE BUILDING BLOCKS OF LIFE: BIOLOGY

1. **Photosynthesis: Nature's Solar-Powered Factories** - Plants are like little green factories that use sunlight to make their food in a process called photosynthesis. It's as if they have tiny solar panels on their leaves, turning sunlight into a delicious sugar snack, all while giving us fresh oxygen as a thank-you note.

2. **The Human Heart: Your Personal Drummer** - Your heart beats about 100,000 times a day, pumping blood all around your body like a dedicated drummer keeping the rhythm in a band. It's your very own drum solo that plays non-stop, making sure your body's rock concert can go on day and night.

3. **Butterflies: The Ultimate Makeover Artists**
   - Butterflies start their lives as caterpillars before spinning cocoons and emerging as flying works of art. It's the animal kingdom's most dramatic makeover, turning a little crawler into a sky dancer with wings that could win any fashion show.

4. **Sharks: The Oceans' Tooth Replacers** - Sharks can grow and lose over 30,000 teeth in their lifetime. They have rows of spare teeth just waiting for their turn, making them the ultimate tooth fairies of the sea. It's like having a conveyor belt of teeth, always ready with a sharp smile.

5. **Bacteria: The Tiny Tenants** - Your body is home to trillions of bacteria, with most of them living in your gut and helping you digest food. It's like having tiny roommates who help with the cooking and cleaning, except they're too small to steal your leftovers.

6. **The Octopus: The Ocean's Escape Artist** - Octopuses can squeeze through tiny gaps,

change color, and even use tools, making them
the ocean's Houdinis. They're like squishy,
eight-armed magicians, always ready with
a trick up their sleeve (or rather, their
tentacle).

7. **Giraffes: The Tallest Heart Pumps** - Giraffes
    have huge hearts that can weigh up to 25
    pounds, necessary to pump blood all the way
    up to their brains. It's as if they're walking
    around with a love for heights, literally
    wearing their hearts on their long, long
    sleeves.

8. **Honeybees: Nature's Mathematicians** -
    Honeybees use the hexagon to build their
    honeycombs because it's the most efficient
    shape, fitting together perfectly without
    wasting any space. Bees are like tiny
    architects, buzzing about their calculations to
    make sure every drop of honey has a sweet
    home.

9. **Chameleons: The Quick-Change Artists** -
    Chameleons can change their color to blend

into their surroundings or communicate.
They're the masters of disguise, capable
of changing their outfits in a blink, making
them the original mood rings of the animal
kingdom.

10. **The Venus Flytrap: The Hungry Plant** - The
Venus Flytrap catches its meals by snapping
shut on unsuspecting insects, using one of
nature's coolest traps. It's like having a plant
with a mouth, dining on bugs with a side of
photosynthesis.

11. **Ants: The Super Lifters** - Ants can lift
objects many times their own weight, like
tiny bodybuilders showing off at the gym. If
you were as strong as an ant, you could lift
a car over your head, no sweat (but maybe a
little strain).

12. **The Gecko's Sticky Feet: Nature's Suction
Cups** - Geckos can climb smooth surfaces
thanks to tiny hairs on their feet that act
like suction cups. They're like the world's
tiniest superheroes, scaling walls and ceilings

without a web or cape in sight.

13. **Penguins: The Belly-Sliding Birds** - Penguins can't fly, but they're experts at belly sliding on ice and swimming fast in water. They're like the comedians of the bird world, choosing to slide into their DMs (Dinner Meetings) on their stomachs.

14. **Turtles: The Ancient Mariners** - Some turtles have been around the oceans for over 100 million years, making them some of the oldest travelers on Earth. They're like the great-great-grandparents of the sea, carrying ancient stories on their backs, along with a home that's always travel-ready.

15. **The Axolotl: The Regeneration Champion** - Axolotls can regrow lost body parts, including their heart and brain. It's like they have a magic potion for healing, making them the wizards of the animal kingdom, always ready for a quick fix.

16. **The Platypus: Nature's Oddball** - The platypus lays eggs, has a duck's bill, a beaver's tail, and uses electricity to find its food. It's like nature mixed up its blueprints and ended up with an animal that's a living, swimming, electric puzzle.

17. **The Peacock's Tail: The Ultimate Showoff** - A peacock's tail feathers can fan out to display a stunning pattern used to attract mates. It's like having a built-in dance floor and disco ball, ready to impress with the shake of a tail.

18. **Bats: The Nighttime Navigators** - Bats use echolocation to see in the dark, sending out sound waves that bounce back to them. They're like the night's sonar experts, navigating the dark with sound selfies that help them "see" their way around.

19. **The Mimic Octopus: The Impersonator of the Sea** - The mimic octopus can imitate other sea creatures to avoid predators. It's like the ocean's actor, ready to take on any

role from a venomous lionfish to a harmless sea snake, all without a script.

20. **Human Fingerprints: The Unique Identifier** - Every person's fingerprints are unique, not even identical twins share the same patterns. It's like having your own personal barcode, but instead of scanning for prices, it's used for high-fives and leaving sneaky marks on foggy windows.

21. **Photosynthesis vs. Respiration: Nature's Breath In, Breath Out** - Plants do something super cool called photosynthesis, where they take in sunlight and turn it into food, breathing out oxygen for us to inhale. Then we, along with animals, take a deep breath, use up that oxygen, and breathe out carbon dioxide, which plants then use again. It's like a cosmic game of tag between us and plants, passing back and forth the breath of life.

22. **Cells: The Building Blocks of Life** - Every living thing is made up of tiny units called cells, kind of like how every castle is made up

of individual bricks. But cells are way cooler because they can eat, grow, and even make mini versions of themselves. Imagine if your LEGO bricks could do that!

23. **DNA: Nature's Recipe Book** - DNA is like a cookbook that holds all the recipes for making you uniquely you, from your hair color to your toe shape. It's packed with instructions for everything about every living thing. If you could read your DNA, it would be like flipping through the story of you, written in a code of As, Ts, Gs, and Cs.

24. **The Water Cycle: Earth's Never-Ending Water Ride** - The water cycle is like the Earth playing with its water toys, evaporating water from oceans and lakes, forming clouds, and then raining it back down again. It's a never-ending loop that keeps the planet's water in constant motion, like a giant, splashy merry-go-round.

25. **Fungi: The Decomposers** - Fungi are nature's cleanup crew, breaking down dead stuff and

turning it into soil. They're like the recyclers of the natural world, taking fallen leaves and old logs and turning them into new life. Without them, we'd be up to our necks in dead things!

26. **Viruses: The Tiny Invaders** - Viruses are super tiny, not even alive in the usual sense, but when they sneak into living cells, they can make copies of themselves. It's like they're tiny pirates hijacking your cells to make more pirates, leading to all sorts of chaos, like the common cold or flu.

27. **Ecosystems: Nature's Networks** - An ecosystem is a community of living things all interacting with each other and their environment, like a big, natural, bustling city. There are forests, oceans, deserts, and even your backyard - each with its own set of residents and rules. It's like the Earth is made up of different neighborhoods, each with its unique character.

28. **The Immune System: The Body's Defense Force** - Your immune system is like your body's superhero team, fighting off germs and viruses that try to make you sick. White blood cells are the heroes, rushing to the scene of an invasion and battling the bad guys to keep you healthy. It's like having an action movie happening inside you all the time!

29. **Plants' Defense Mechanisms: Nature's Booby Traps** - Some plants have developed crazy ways to protect themselves from being eaten, like cacti with their sharp spikes or Venus flytraps that snap shut on bugs. It's as if these plants have set up their own booby traps, ready to defend themselves against any salad-loving intruders.

30. **The Brain's Neuroplasticity: The Ultimate Learner** - The brain's ability to change and adapt, known as neuroplasticity, is like having a superpower that lets you keep learning and getting better at things your whole life. It's as if your brain is made of playdough, constantly reshaping itself to become smarter and stronger, no matter how old you get.

31. **The Nitrogen Cycle: Nature's Recycling System** - The nitrogen cycle is how nature recycles nitrogen, a vital ingredient for plant life. It's a complex tag team involving the air, soil, plants, and even lightning, ensuring that all living things have the nutrients they need to grow. It's like the Earth has its own garden composting system, but way more high-tech.

32. **Bioluminescence: Nature's Glow Sticks** - Some creatures, like fireflies and deep-sea fish, can make their own light, a trick called bioluminescence. It's as if they carry around their own natural glow sticks, lighting up to find mates or scare off predators. Imagine if you could light up your room just by flicking your wrist!

33. **The Symbiotic Relationships: Nature's Teamwork** - Symbiosis is when different species live together and help each other out, like clownfish that live safely among anemone tentacles, or bees that pollinate flowers while getting nectar. It's like having a best friend in nature who's always got your back, proving that teamwork can happen in the most

unexpected places.

34. **Mitochondria: The Powerhouses of the Cell**
- Mitochondria are like tiny power stations inside your cells, turning food into energy so you can run, jump, and play. It's as if every cell has its own battery pack, ready to charge up and power through the day's adventures.

35. **Evolution: Nature's Experiment with Life**
- Evolution is how living things change over generations, adapting to their environment, like how giraffes got long necks to reach high leaves. It's like nature is constantly tinkering and experimenting, trying out new looks and skills to see what works best in the game of survival.

36. **The Coral Reefs: The Rainforests of the Sea** - Coral reefs are bustling underwater cities, teeming with colorful fish, plants, and creatures. They're like the bustling metropolises of the ocean, offering food, shelter, and some of the most vibrant

neighborhoods you'll ever see, all built by tiny coral polyps working together.

37. **Seed Dispersal: Nature's Way of Planting Trees** - Plants have clever ways to spread their seeds, like dandelions that use the wind, or fruits eaten by animals who then carry the seeds away. It's as if plants are launching their own little astronauts into the world, hoping they'll land in a spot perfect for growing a new life.

38. **The Human Genome: The Blueprint of You** - The human genome is the complete set of instructions for making you, stored in DNA. It's like having a personal blueprint that tells you everything from how tall you'll grow to the color of your eyes, making each person a unique construction project based on a very special set of plans.

39. **Animal Migration: The Ultimate Road Trip** - Many animals take epic journeys, migrating thousands of miles to find food, warmer weather, or a place to have babies. It's like

they're going on the ultimate road trip, but without GPS, relying instead on instincts, the stars, or the Earth's magnetic field to guide them.

40. **Pollen: Nature's Fertilizer** - Pollen is how plants reproduce, carried by the wind or by animals from one flower to another. It's like sending love letters between plants, hoping to start new life. Without it, we wouldn't have many of the fruits and vegetables we love to eat.

41. **The Skin: Your Body's Suit of Armor** - Your skin is your body's largest organ, protecting you from germs and the sun's rays, keeping you warm or cool, and letting you feel the world through touch. It's like wearing a suit of armor that's also super smart, constantly adjusting to keep you safe and comfortable.

42. **Animal Camouflage: The Masters of Hide and Seek** - Some animals are so good at blending into their surroundings, they become almost invisible. It's like they have a natural

invisibility cloak, making them the champions
of hide and seek, whether they're avoiding
predators or sneaking up on prey.

43. **The Stomach: Your Personal Food Processor**
    - The stomach uses acids and enzymes to
    break down food, turning it into energy and
    nutrients your body can use. It's like having
    a personal food processor inside you, mushing
    up pizza and apples into something your cells
    can snack on.

44. **Plant Hormones: Nature's Chemical
    Messengers** - Just like animals, plants use
    hormones to send messages within themselves,
    controlling growth, flowering, and even how
    they respond to light and gravity. It's as if
    plants have their own internal text messaging
    system, keeping all parts updated on what
    they need to do.

45. **The Blood: Your Body's Delivery Service -**
    Blood carries oxygen, nutrients, and more all
    around your body, like a delivery service that
    never takes a break. It's like having a fleet

of trucks on an endless road trip through your veins, making sure every cell gets the supplies it needs.

46. **The Lungs: Your Personal Air Filters** - The lungs pull in oxygen from the air and get rid of carbon dioxide from your body. They're like a pair of personal air filters, making sure you get all the fresh air you need for those deep breaths or long sighs.

47. **Biodiversity: Earth's Tapestry of Life** - Biodiversity is the variety of life on Earth, from tiny microbes to giant whales. It's like Earth is wearing a tapestry woven from every kind of living thread, creating a picture so complex and beautiful, it's beyond imagination. It's up to us to keep adding to it, not letting any threads unravel.

48. **The Brain's Learning Switch: The Curiosity Button** - Scientists discovered that our brains have something like a learning switch that flips on when we're curious about something new. It's like your brain has a

big, shiny "Curiosity" button, and when you press it, learning becomes as easy as eating your favorite slice of cake. So, every time you ask "why" or "how," you're basically a brainy superhero, powering up for your next adventure in knowledge!

49. **The Deciduous Trees' Seasonal Wardrobe: Nature's Fashionistas** - Deciduous trees change their leaves with the seasons, showcasing a dazzling array of colors from vibrant green to fiery red and golden yellow before taking a winter break. It's as if they have the most extensive wardrobe in nature, deciding to throw a fashion show every year to remind us how stylish the natural world can be. And when they're done with one look, they just let it drop and start planning their next season's outfit.

50. **The Digestive Dance: Your Guts' Groovy Moves** - The digestive system doesn't just break down food; it literally moves it along in a wave-like motion known as peristalsis, kind of like doing the wave at a sports game. Imagine a tiny disco happening inside you,

where your intestines groove and shimmy to
make sure your meals hit all the right dance
floors from your stomach to... the grand exit.

Chapter 3

THE POWER OF ELEMENTS: CHEMISTRY

1. **Atoms: The Universe's Building Blocks** – Atoms are like tiny Lego pieces that make up everything around us. Imagine if your toys could be rearranged to make anything from a banana to a bicycle. That's what atoms do, combining in countless ways to create everything in the world!

2. **Water: The Shape-Shifting Liquid** – Water is a magical substance that can exist as a liquid, solid (ice), or gas (steam). It's like having a superhero that can change shape, going from being the perfect drink to the coolest ice sculpture or floating away as an invisible vapor.

3. **Oxygen: The Breath of Life** - Oxygen is the gas we all breathe in to stay alive, and it makes up about 21% of the air. It's like an invisible friend that keeps us dancing, running, and playing. Without it, we'd be more bored than on a rainy day with no internet!

4. **Carbon Dioxide: The Plant Snack** - Carbon dioxide is a gas we breathe out, and plants use it to make their food. When we exhale, it's like we're sending a snack in the air for plants, who then throw us a 'thank you' party by making oxygen. Talk about great teamwork!

5. **Acids and Bases: The Chemistry Opposites** - Acids and bases are like the superheroes and villains of chemistry. Vinegar is an acid, and baking soda is a base. When they meet, they react and create a fizzy explosion, perfect for homemade volcanoes but not for brushing your teeth!

6. **The Periodic Table: Chemistry's Treasure Map** - The Periodic Table is a chart where all the different atoms (elements) are listed. It's

like a treasure map for scientists, showing
them all the ingredients available to make
everything from medicines to moon rocks.

7. **Photosynthesis: The Green Magic -**
Photosynthesis is not just about plants making
food; it's a chemical reaction where they take
water, carbon dioxide, and sunlight to create
oxygen and sugars. It's like plants are little
green magicians, turning sunbeams and air
into life.

8. **Salt: The Flavorful Mineral** - Table salt is a
chemical made of two elements: sodium and
chlorine. When they join, they make our fries
tasty! It's like two boring individuals joining
a band and suddenly creating the hit song of
the year.

9. **Rust: Iron's Battle with Air** - Rust happens
when iron reacts with oxygen in the air,
especially if there's water around. It's like
iron is battling with the air, and rust is the
scar it gets when it loses. That's why your
bike gets rusty if you leave it out in the rain.

10. **Soap: The Dirt Fighter** - Soap cleans by making water better at washing away dirt and oil. It's like a superhero for water, giving it superpowers to fight the Evil Dirt King and his Grease Goblin minions, making everything from your hands to your shirts sparkling clean.

11. **Helium: The Floating Gas** - Helium is a gas that's lighter than air, which is why balloons filled with it float up. It's like filling a balloon with tiny invisible birds that just want to fly to the ceiling. Plus, if you breathe a little in (with an adult's help!), it makes your voice squeaky!

12. **Chemical Reactions: Nature's Tiny Explosions** - A chemical reaction is when different substances come together and make something new, like vinegar and baking soda making a volcano erupt. It's like a dance party for atoms where they swap partners and create a show.

13. **Plastics: The Shape-Shifting Materials**
- Plastics are made from long chains of molecules called polymers. They can be molded into almost anything, from toys to bottles. It's like having a magical dough that can become whatever you want, but remember, it doesn't like to break down, so recycle!

14. **Alloys: Metal Team-Ups** - Alloys are mixtures of different metals, like steel, which is mostly iron with a bit of carbon. It's like metals having a potluck dinner, where everyone brings something to the table, creating a dish (or in this case, a metal) that's stronger and better.

15. **The Noble Gases: The Loner Elements** - Noble gases, like neon and argon, don't usually react with other elements. They're like the cool loners of the periodic table, glowing when electrically charged but otherwise keeping to themselves, not causing any drama.

16. **Caffeine: The Wake-Up Molecule** - Caffeine, found in coffee and tea, is a chemical that

can make you feel more awake and alert. It's like a tiny alarm clock for your brain, saying, "Hey! Wake up and smell the coffee... or the tea... or the cola!"

17. **Sugar: The Sweet Crystals** - Sugar, a sweet-tasting carbohydrate, is made of carbon, hydrogen, and oxygen. It's like nature's candy, giving us quick energy and making things like cookies and ice cream taste delicious (but too much can lead to a sugar rush, so balance is key!).

18. **Limestone: The Sea's Memory** - Limestone is a rock often made from the remains of ancient sea creatures' shells. It's like the ocean's memory book, storing tales of long-gone creatures in stone. If rocks could talk, limestone would have the best stories.

19. **Chlorophyll: The Green Color Machine** - Chlorophyll is the chemical that gives plants their green color and helps them make food. It's like plants have their own green paint that also cooks their meals using sunlight.

Talk about multitasking!

20. **Glue: The Sticky Solution** - Glue is a sticky substance that can hold things together, made from polymers that grab onto surfaces. It's like having a liquid sidekick that helps you fix broken toys, seal envelopes, and even create art, all while sticking to the task at hand.

21. **Baking Soda & Vinegar: The Fizzing Duo** - When baking soda meets vinegar, they throw a fizzy party that can power up a homemade volcano or inflate a balloon. It's like they're saying, "Let's throw some bubbles and see how much fun we can make!" This reaction is a classic science fair star, showing off the exciting action when an acid and a base become friends.

21. **Water Molecules: The Stick Together Squad** - Water molecules are super social, always sticking together because of something called hydrogen bonding. It's like each water molecule holds hands with its neighbors, making water liquid at room temperature and

giving it the ability to climb up thin tubes in plants. If water molecules were kids, they'd be the best at playing Red Rover.

22. **Chlorine: The Pool Cleaner** - Chlorine is used to keep swimming pools clean, not by scrubbing the sides, but by breaking down bacteria and germs in the water. It's like having a microscopic pool lifeguard that blows the whistle on any dirt trying to ruin your swim. Just remember, too much can make your eyes red, like it's saying, "I've got my eyes on you, germs!"

23. **The States of Matter: The Transforming Trio** - Matter comes in three main states: solid, liquid, and gas. It's like a magician that can transform water into ice, steam, or keep it as a refreshing drink, depending on the temperature. This shape-shifting act is all about adding or taking away energy, like deciding whether to chill out, go with the flow, or let off some steam.

24. **Acid Rain: The Unwanted Weather** - Acid rain happens when pollution from cars and

factories mixes with rain, making it slightly acidic. It's like the clouds are crying tears that are a bit grumpy, affecting plants, animals, and buildings. The Earth prefers its showers plain, without any extra pollution seasoning.

25. **Enzymes: Nature's Speedy Helpers -** Enzymes are like the speedy delivery workers of the cell, helping chemical reactions happen faster. Without them, our bodies would move at a snail's pace, turning eating a sandwich into a day-long event. They're the unsung heroes who make sure everything in our body works as fast as it should.

26. **Fluorescence: The Glow-in-the-Dark Trick** - Some substances can absorb light and then re-emit it, glowing in stunning colors. This trick, called fluorescence, is like having a secret message that only shows up under a special light, turning your room into a disco party or revealing the hidden beauty of minerals and sea creatures.

27. **Carbon: The Element of Life** – Carbon is a key ingredient in all living things, making it a superstar element. It's like the Lego block that's used in every set, from building the DNA double helix to making up the gasses that plants love. Without carbon, life's construction kit would be missing its most important piece.

28. **pH Scale: The Acid-Base Meter** – The pH scale measures how acidic or basic a solution is, from stomach acid to baking soda. It's like a scoreboard at a sports game, telling you if Team Acid or Team Base is winning, with pure water always playing a fair game right in the middle.

29. **Gold: The Unreactive Treasure** – Gold is famous not just because it's shiny, but because it hardly ever reacts with other elements. This makes it super special in chemistry and why it's treasured in jewelry and electronics. It's like the cool kid that's friendly with everyone but doesn't get into any trouble.

30. **Photosensitive Chemicals: Sunlight's Artistic Touch** - Some chemicals change when exposed to light, a process used in photography and sun-sensitive paper. It's like these chemicals are playing shadow tag, capturing the silhouette of whatever blocks the light. With just a flash of sunlight, they freeze a moment in time or create beautiful patterns.

31. **The Chemistry of Cooking: The Edible Experiments** - Cooking is like doing a tasty chemistry experiment where heat, mixing, and chemical reactions turn ingredients into delicious meals. Whether it's the browning of toast or the thickening of gravy, it's all delicious chemistry in action, proving that even in the kitchen, science rules!

32. **Insulation: Keeping the Temperature Just Right** - Insulators are materials that don't let heat escape easily, like the wool in your sweater. They're like cozy blankets, keeping the warm in and the cold out. Thanks to insulation, we can enjoy warm meals and snowball fights without turning into human popsicles.

33. **The Periodic Table's Organization: Elements in Order** - The Periodic Table isn't just a random list; it's organized by properties, from gases to metals to noble gases. It's like a library where every book (element) has its perfect spot, making it easy for scientists to find the stories (properties) they're interested in.

34. **Polymers: The Long Chains of Chemistry** - Polymers are long chains of molecules, found in everything from plastic bags to DNA. It's like the beads on a necklace, where each bead is a small molecule, and when you string them together, you get something much bigger and often more interesting.

35. **Ozone Layer: Earth's Sunscreen** - The ozone layer acts like Earth's sunscreen, protecting us from the sun's harmful UV rays. Without it, we'd get sunburned way easier, and it would be harmful to all living things. It's like a giant, invisible umbrella that keeps us all safe from getting too crispy under the sun.

36. **Chemical Bonds: The Glue of the Atom World** - Chemical bonds are what hold atoms together in molecules, like glue holding together a model airplane. Whether it's a water molecule or the proteins in your body, these bonds are the reason everything doesn't just fall apart into atomic dust.

37. **Catalysts: The Reaction Cheerleaders** - Catalysts are substances that help speed up chemical reactions without getting used up. They're like cheerleaders for chemical reactions, encouraging them to go faster and be more efficient, proving that sometimes, a little encouragement goes a long way.

38. **The Greenhouse Effect: Earth's Warm Blanket** - The greenhouse effect is like Earth's warm blanket, trapping heat from the sun to keep our planet cozy. Without it, Earth would be too cold for us. But too much of this blanket, and we start to overheat, showing that even with blankets, there can be too much of a good thing.

39. **Vitamins: The Body's Tiny Helpers** - Vitamins are like tiny helpers that our bodies need to stay healthy, doing everything from keeping our bones strong to helping us see in the dark. They're part of nature's toolkit, ensuring that the complex machinery of our bodies runs smoothly.

40. **Baking Soda & Vinegar: The Fizzing Duo** - When baking soda meets vinegar, they throw a fizzy party that can power up a homemade volcano or inflate a balloon. It's like they're saying, "Let's throw some bubbles and see how much fun we can make!" This reaction is a classic science fair star, showing off the exciting action when an acid and a base become friends.

41. **Water Molecules: The Stick Together Squad** - Water molecules are super social, always sticking together because of something called hydrogen bonding. It's like each water molecule holds hands with its neighbors, making water liquid at room temperature and giving it the ability to climb up thin tubes in plants. If water molecules were kids, they'd

be the best at playing Red Rover.

42.   **Chlorine: The Pool Cleaner** – Chlorine is used to keep swimming pools clean, not by scrubbing the sides, but by breaking down bacteria and germs in the water. It's like having a microscopic pool lifeguard that blows the whistle on any dirt trying to ruin your swim. Just remember, too much can make your eyes red, like it's saying, "I've got my eyes on you, germs!"

43.   **The States of Matter: The Transforming Trio** – Matter comes in three main states: solid, liquid, and gas. It's like a magician that can transform water into ice, steam, or keep it as a refreshing drink, depending on the temperature. This shape-shifting act is all about adding or taking away energy, like deciding whether to chill out, go with the flow, or let off some steam.

44.   **Acid Rain: The Unwanted Weather** – Acid rain happens when pollution from cars and factories mixes with rain, making it slightly

acidic. It's like the clouds are crying tears that are a bit grumpy, affecting plants, animals, and buildings. The Earth prefers its showers plain, without any extra pollution seasoning.

45. **Enzymes: Nature's Speedy Helpers -** Enzymes are like the speedy delivery workers of the cell, helping chemical reactions happen faster. Without them, our bodies would move at a snail's pace, turning eating a sandwich into a day-long event. They're the unsung heroes who make sure everything in our body works as fast as it should.

46. **Fluorescence: The Glow-in-the-Dark Trick** - Some substances can absorb light and then re-emit it, glowing in stunning colors. This trick, called fluorescence, is like having a secret message that only shows up under a special light, turning your room into a disco party or revealing the hidden beauty of minerals and sea creatures.

47. **Carbon: The Element of Life** - Carbon is a key ingredient in all living things, making it a superstar element. It's like the Lego block that's used in every set, from building the DNA double helix to making up the gasses that plants love. Without carbon, life's construction kit would be missing its most important piece.

48. **pH Scale: The Acid-Base Meter** - The pH scale measures how acidic or basic a solution is, from stomach acid to baking soda. It's like a scoreboard at a sports game, telling you if Team Acid or Team Base is winning, with pure water always playing a fair game right in the middle.

49. **Gold: The Unreactive Treasure** - Gold is famous not just because it's shiny, but because it hardly ever reacts with other elements. This makes it super special in chemistry and why it's treasured in jewelry and electronics. It's like the cool kid that's friendly with everyone but doesn't get into any trouble.

50. **Nitrogen:** The Invisible Giant – Nitrogen is a gas that makes up about 78% of the Earth's atmosphere, far more than oxygen. It's like an invisible giant, quietly supporting life by helping plants grow. Without it, the air we breathe and the food we eat would not be the same. Nitrogen is part of the great cycle of life, moving from the air to the soil, into living organisms, and back again, playing a key role in both the beginning and the nourishment of life on Earth.

Chapter 4

THE FORCE OF NATURE: PHYSICS

1. **Gravity: The Invisible Hug** - Gravity is like the Earth giving us a gentle hug, keeping us from floating off into space. Without it, we'd be the real "Space Jam"!

2. **Magnets: The Attraction Masters** - Magnets are like the popular kids in the playground. Some things are drawn to them, while others don't stick around.

3. **The Bouncy Ball Theory** - When you bounce a ball, it doesn't come all the way back up because of gravity and energy loss. It's like the ball gets tired too!

4. **Light: The Speedy Traveler** - Light travels so fast, it could go around the Earth 7.5 times in one second. If light raced a snail, the snail wouldn't even know the race started!

5. **Sound: The Invisible Messenger** - Sound travels through the air by making molecules vibrate. It's like when you're playing telephone with invisible string cans!

6. **Electricity: The Power Stream** - Electricity is the flow of tiny particles called electrons. It's like a river of energy flowing through wires!

7. **The Rainbow Recipe** - Rainbows happen when sunlight gets bent and split into colors by raindrops. It's nature's way of painting the sky!

8. **The Moon's Tidal Power** - The Moon's gravity pulls on the Earth's oceans, causing tides. Like the Moon is playing tug-of-war with the sea!

9. **The Floating Balloon Trick** - Helium balloons float because helium is lighter than air. It's like filling a balloon with the secret of flight!

10. **Friction: The Party Pooper** - Friction is what stops your slide fun. It's the invisible hand that says, "Slow down, buddy!"

11. **The Echo Echo** - An echo happens when sound bounces off a surface and returns to you. It's nature's way of copying your homework.

12. **The Leaning Tower of Pisa Experiment** - Galileo supposedly dropped two balls of different weights from the Leaning Tower of Pisa to show they'd land at the same time. Physics doesn't play favorites!

13. **The Dancing Shadows** - Shadows change size and shape during the day because of the Sun's position. It's like playing shadow tag with the Sun!

14. **Static Electricity: The Hair Raiser** -
Rubbing a balloon on your hair creates static
electricity, making your hair stand up. It's the
balloon's way of saying, "I'm electric!"

15. **The Northern Lights Show** - The Northern
Lights are caused by particles from the Sun
hitting Earth's atmosphere. It's like Earth's
own neon sign.

16. **The Hot Air Rises Rule** - Hot air rises
because it's lighter than cool air. It's like the
warm air is escaping to a no-kids-allowed
party in the sky.

17. **The Invisible Force Field** - The Earth's
magnetic field protects us from solar wind.
It's like having an invisible superhero shield
around the planet.

18. **The Speedy Sound Barrier** - Breaking the
sound barrier means moving faster than
sound. It's like saying, "Excuse me, sound,

coming through!"

19. **Water's Weird Boiling Point** - Water boils at a lower temperature the higher you are. On Mount Everest, you could boil water at a cool party temperature!

20. **The Zero-Gravity Illusion** - Astronauts float in space not because there's no gravity but because they're in free fall around the Earth. It's like the ultimate "no floor" game.

21. **The Solar Powerhouse** - The Sun is a massive ball of gas that gives off energy. It's like a giant, never-ending power battery in the sky.

22. **The Light Bulb Moment** - Thomas Edison didn't invent the first light bulb, but he made one that lasted longer. It's like he said, "Let there be light, but let it stick around for a while!"

23. **The Mirror Image Mystery** - Mirrors flip images horizontally but not vertically. It's like they're playing a prank on your reflection.

24. **The Curious Case of Curved Space** - Gravity can bend space and time. It's like space is a funhouse mirror making things wobble.

25. **The Unstoppable Force Meets the Immovable Object** - When an unstoppable force meets an immovable object, physics gets a headache. It's the ultimate "What if?"

26. **The Slinky Drop** - Dropping a Slinky seems to defy gravity because the bottom doesn't fall until the top catches up. It's like the Slinky is saying, "Nope, not moving yet!"

27. **The Colorful Soap Bubble** - Soap bubbles show colors because of light waves interfering with each other. It's like the bubble is wearing a rainbow dress.

28. **The Moon's Illusion** - The Moon looks bigger near the horizon due to a trick of the mind. It's like the Moon is playing dress-up with the Earth.

29. **The Perpetual Pendulum** - A pendulum keeps swinging because of inertia, but eventually, friction slows it down. It's like it's saying, "I could do this all day... or at least for a little while."

30. **The Invisible Air** - Air takes up space even though we can't see it. It's like having an invisible friend who's always there for you.

31. **The Pressure Cooker Effect** - Pressure increases the boiling point of water, making food cook faster in a pressure cooker. It's like a speed boost for cooking!

32. **The Ice-Skating Glide** - Ice skating works because the skates melt the ice a little, reducing friction. It's like having a tiny water

slide under your feet.

33. **The X-ray Vision** - X-rays can see through your skin but not your bones. It's like having superhero vision, but only for the skeleton.

34. **The Ping-Pong Float** - Ping-pong balls float in water because they're filled with air, making them less dense. It's like they're wearing tiny life jackets.

35. **The Chocolate Melting Mystery** - Chocolate melts in your mouth because it's just below body temperature. It's like the chocolate is saying, "Ahh, perfect!"

36. **The Balancing Act** - You can balance better with your eyes open because of your inner ear and vision working together. It's like having built-in stabilizers.

37. **The Refracting Prism** - A prism breaks light into a rainbow by bending the light. It's like a magic wand for light!

38. **The Spinning Earth** - The Earth spins at about 1,000 miles per hour, but we don't feel it because we're moving with it. It's like being on a merry-go-round that's perfectly smooth.

39. **The Humming High Tension Wires** - High tension wires hum because of the vibration of electricity passing through them. It's like the wires are trying to sing.

40. **The Fading Sunburn** - Sunburn fades as your skin sheds its damaged cells. It's like your skin saying, "Let's forget that happened."

41. **The Bending Spoon Illusion** - Bending a spoon with your mind is a magic trick, not physics. But physics can explain how the trick works!

42. **The Camera Obscura Effect** - A dark room with a small hole can project outside scenes onto a wall. It's like having a live painting.

43. **The Whistling Tea Kettle** - A tea kettle whistles because steam forces its way through a small opening. It's like the kettle is politely saying, "I'm ready!"

44. **The Quantum Leap** - In quantum physics, particles can jump from one energy level to another instantaneously. It's like playing cosmic hopscotch.

45. **The See-saw Principle** - A seesaw works on the principle of balance. It's like finding the sweet spot between too much and too little.

46. **The Hot Chocolate Effect** - Stirring hot chocolate and then tapping the cup makes it sound different because of bubbles. It's like the cocoa is tuning its own instrument.

47. **The Lightning Rod Attraction** - Lightning rods protect buildings by attracting lightning. It's like having a superhero shield for storms.

48. **The Warming Greenhouse Effect** - The greenhouse effect warms the Earth because gases trap heat. It's like Earth wearing a cozy blanket.

49. **The Invisible Wi-Fi** - Wi-Fi uses radio waves to send data invisibly. It's like having an invisible mailman delivering emails.

50. **The Unbreakable Egg Drop** - Dropping an egg onto a pillow without breaking it shows inertia and force distribution. It's like the egg is getting a soft hug!

Chapter 5

INNOVATIONS IN TECHNOLOGY

1. **Smartphones: The Tiny Wizards in Our Pockets** – Smartphones are like tiny magic wands that let us talk to people far away, answer any question, and even watch movies. Imagine having a little wizard in your pocket that can do almost anything you ask, from waking you up to playing your favorite song!

2. **The Internet: The Invisible Library of Everything** – The Internet is an invisible, giant library where you can find the answer to any question, learn how to make slime, or watch videos of cats doing funny things. It's like having a magic book that never ends, always has new pages to turn, and never needs a bookmark.

3. **Electric Cars: The Silent Speedsters** - Electric cars are like superheroes of the road, running on electricity instead of gasoline, and moving so quietly they can sneak up like ninjas. They're Earth's friends, helping keep the air clean so we can all breathe easier during our outdoor adventures.

4. **Video Games: The Portals to Other Worlds** - Video games are like magic portals that take you to other worlds where you can be a knight, a space explorer, or even a farmer. It's like jumping into a painting and living out an adventure, except you get to control the action with just the push of a button.

5. **Robots: Our Helpful Mechanical Friends** - Robots can do all sorts of things, from building cars to cleaning floors and even exploring other planets. Imagine having a robot buddy that could do your chores, give you piggyback rides, and never gets tired of playing hide and seek.

6. **Virtual Reality: The Imagination Expander** - Virtual reality (VR) headsets can take you to places you've never imagined, from the bottom of the ocean to the surface of Mars, all from your living room. It's like wearing a pair of magical goggles that can transport you to any world you want to explore.

7. **3D Printing: The Dream Maker Machine** - 3D printers can create toys, tools, and even parts for space rockets, layer by layer. Imagine a machine that can make almost anything you draw, like a genie that turns your drawings into real, hold-in-your-hand objects.

8. **Renewable Energy: Nature's Power Plants** - Solar panels and wind turbines use the sun and wind to make electricity. It's like having giant gadgets that soak up nature's energy, turning sunny days and breezy afternoons into power for playing video games or keeping the lights on.

9. **Drones: The Flying Cameras** - Drones are like remote-controlled birds that can take pictures

and videos from the sky. Imagine sending up your own little helicopter to spy on what birds see when they fly, or to take a selfie from above your backyard.

10. **Artificial Intelligence: The Brainy Computers** - Artificial intelligence (AI) is when computers are taught to think and learn like humans. It's like having a robot friend who's really good at games, can help with homework, and sometimes, gets a little too good at predicting what you're going to do next.

11. **The Cloud: The Invisible Backpack** - "The Cloud" is where we can store our photos, documents, and music online instead of on our devices. It's like having an invisible backpack that follows you everywhere, holding all your stuff so you can reach in and grab what you need, anytime, without carrying the weight.

12. **GPS: The Global Treasure Map** - GPS systems help us find our way anywhere on Earth, like modern-day treasure maps that fit in our pockets. Whether you're hunting for buried

treasure or just trying to find the nearest pizza place, GPS is like having a compass that talks and can guide you street by street.

13. **Touchscreens: The Tap-and-Swipe Magic -** Touchscreens let us tap, swipe, and pinch to control our gadgets with our fingertips. It's like having a magic screen that responds to your touch, turning taps into commands, as if you're a wizard casting spells to make things happen.

14. **Social Media: The Global Gathering Place -** Social media is like a huge online playground where you can share pictures, stories, and chat with friends and family, no matter how far away they are. It's like sending digital messages in a bottle across the vast ocean of the internet, always finding their way to the right person.

15. **Streaming Services: The Endless Movie Marathon -** Streaming services let us watch movies and shows whenever we want, turning our homes into personal movie theaters. It's

like having a magic box that plays any movie you can think of, on demand, without ever needing to rewind the tape.

16. **E-books: The Library in Your Hand** - E-books are digital versions of books that you can read on a device, carrying a whole library in your hand. Imagine if your backpack could hold thousands of books, but didn't weigh more than a feather, and you could flip through them with a tap.

17. **Wearable Technology: The Smart Accessories** - Wearable technology, like smartwatches, can tell you the time, track your steps, and even send messages. It's like wearing a tiny computer as a watch or a bracelet, making you feel like a secret agent on a mission.

18. **Augmented Reality: The World, Upgraded** - Augmented reality (AR) adds digital images to the real world, like seeing a dinosaur in your living room through your phone. It's like having magic glasses that overlay cartoons or information on top of what you're

already seeing, making everyday a bit more
extraordinary.

19. **The Internet of Things: The Talkative
Appliances** - The Internet of Things (IoT) is
when everyday objects, like fridges, lamps,
and thermostats, are connected online and can
communicate. It's like your toaster and fridge
having a chat about what you're going to have
for breakfast, making life a little easier and a
lot more futuristic.

20. **Space Exploration Technology: The Final
Frontier Tools** - Technology that allows us
to explore space, like rockets and satellites,
helps us understand the universe. It's like
building a giant slingshot that can send
cameras and robots to outer space, bringing
back pictures and data from places we've only
dreamed of visiting.

21. **Coding: The Language of Computers** - Coding
is like teaching your computer how to do
new tricks, from making games to building
websites. It's like writing a secret recipe

that tells your computer exactly how to whip up your favorite digital treats, turning your creative ideas into cool projects you can play with on the screen.

22. **Self-Driving Cars: The Autopilot Vehicles** - Self-driving cars are like magic carpets on wheels, using cameras and computers to see the road and make decisions. Imagine hopping into a car that knows where to go and how to get there, all while you sit back, relax, and enjoy the ride, feeling like you're in a sci-fi movie.

23. **Facial Recognition: The Computer's Eye for Faces** - Facial recognition technology helps computers recognize and identify human faces, kind of like how you recognize your friends. It's as if your computer or phone has its own pair of eyes, making it easier to unlock your device or tag photos, but also reminding us to be mindful about privacy.

24. **Biotechnology: Nature Meets Technology** - Biotechnology is when scientists use living

things, like plants and bacteria, to make new products, from medicines to biofuels. It's like having a tiny lab in nature where tiny workers help us solve big problems, showing how technology can work hand in hand with the natural world.

25. **Nanotechnology: The Tiny Tech Revolution** - Nanotechnology deals with super small things, smaller than a human hair, to create new materials and devices. Imagine building with blocks so tiny you can't see them with your eyes alone, but they can make things like stronger materials or tiny robots that could one day help doctors treat diseases.

26. **Blockchain: The Digital Ledger** - Blockchain is a super secure way to keep track of transactions online, like a digital ledger that's almost impossible to hack. It's like having a diary that automatically writes down everything you trade, from virtual pets to game points, and makes sure no one can cheat.

27. **The Mars Rovers: The Red Planet Explorers**
- Mars rovers are like remote-controlled cars, but instead of racing down your driveway, they're exploring Mars, sending back pictures and data. It's as if we've sent little robotic scouts to another world, looking for clues about water, life, and the secrets of the universe.

28. **Quantum Computing: The Mind-Bending Computers** - Quantum computers use the principles of quantum mechanics to process information in ways that regular computers can't. Imagine a computer that can solve super complicated puzzles faster than you can blink, helping us understand everything from the human body to the fabric of the universe.

29. **The Hyperloop: The Super-Speed Travel** - The Hyperloop is a futuristic transportation idea, where pods carry people through tubes at incredible speeds. It's like being shot through a giant straw across long distances, turning hours-long trips into minutes, making the world feel a little smaller and adventures a lot bigger.

30. **Wireless Charging: The Invisible Power Cord** - Wireless charging lets you power up your gadgets without plugging them in, using a special mat or surface. It's like having an invisible power cord that zaps energy right into your devices, keeping them happy and charged up for your next big adventure.

31. **Smart Homes: The Houses That Listen** - Smart homes are equipped with gadgets that let you control lights, temperature, and even locks with your voice or a smartphone. Imagine living in a house that listens and responds, like a friendly robot, making life more convenient and a bit like living in the future.

32. **The Large Hadron Collider: The Particle Smasher** - The Large Hadron Collider is the world's largest and most powerful particle accelerator, used by scientists to smash atoms together and discover new particles. It's like having the ultimate set of building blocks that scientists use to uncover the mysteries of how the universe works, one tiny piece at a time.

33. **Augmented Reality in Education: Learning with a Twist** - Augmented reality (AR) in education lets students see and interact with 3D models right in their classroom, making learning about anything from dinosaurs to the solar system more fun and interactive. It's like having a magic schoolbook that brings lessons to life, turning study time into an adventure.

34. **The Internet of Medical Things: Health Monitoring Made Easy** - The Internet of Medical Things includes devices like smartwatches that monitor your heart rate and apps that track your health. It's like having a tiny doctor on your wrist or phone, keeping an eye on your health and making sure you're at your best every day.

35. **Drones in Agriculture: The Flying Farmers** - Drones are used in farming to survey crops, analyze soil, and even plant seeds. It's like having a bird's-eye view of a farm, where flying robots help farmers grow food more efficiently, proving that technology can help us take care of the Earth and feed more people.

36. **The James Webb Space Telescope: The Universe's Ultimate Spyglass** - The James Webb Space Telescope is designed to look further into space and time than ever before, giving us a glimpse of the first galaxies and stars. It's like having a super-powered spyglass that can see the secrets of the universe, showing us where we all came from.

37. **Voice Assistants: Your Talking Helpers** - Voice assistants like Siri and Alexa can answer questions, play music, and even tell jokes, all with just your voice. It's like having a genie in a speaker, ready to grant your digital wishes and keep you company with a song or a story.

38. **Sustainable Tech: Saving the Planet, One Gadget at a Time** - Sustainable technology includes inventions that help save energy, reduce waste, and protect the environment. It's like Earth's toolbox for fixing climate change, showing that with the right tools, we can build a cleaner, greener future.

39. **3D Bioprinting: Printing Parts for People** - 3D bioprinting is a technology that can print tissues and organs for medical use. Imagine a printer that doesn't use ink or paper, but cells to create things like skin for healing wounds, showing how technology can truly change lives.

40. **Space Tourism: Vacationing Among the Stars** - Space tourism is the idea of traveling to space for fun, not just science. Imagine taking a holiday that's literally out of this world, where you can float in zero gravity and see Earth from a whole new perspective, making it the ultimate adventure for those who have everything.

41. **Digital Art: The Canvas of the Future** - Digital art lets artists use computers and tablets to create masterpieces, from animated movies to stunning illustrations. It's like having a magic paintbrush that never runs out of paint and can undo any mistake with a click, turning the screen into a canvas for endless creativity.

42. **E-Sports: The Digital Arena** - E-sports turn video gaming into competitive sport, where players from around the world battle in virtual arenas for glory and prizes. It's like the Olympics for gamers, proving that with quick reflexes and strategic thinking, playing games can lead to victory laps and gold medals.

43. **Wearable Fitness Trackers: The Personal Coaches** - Wearable fitness trackers monitor your steps, heart rate, and even your sleep, acting like a personal coach on your wrist. They cheer you on to move more, sleep better, and live healthier, making it fun to chase after goals or beat your personal best.

44. **Smart Glasses: The World, Enhanced** - Smart glasses can display information right before your eyes, from directions to messages, without needing to look at a phone. It's like having a secret agent's gadget that whispers secrets only you can see, blending the digital world with the real one.

45. **Driverless Trains: The Autonomous Conductors** - Driverless trains use sensors and automation to safely carry passengers without a human conductor. Imagine hopping on a train that knows exactly where to go, smoothly gliding along tracks like a ghost is at the controls, making commutes more like riding a futuristic carousel.

46. **Gene Editing: Customizing DNA** - Gene editing is like using molecular scissors to tweak the blueprint of life, potentially curing diseases or improving crops. It's like having a tiny editing tool that can correct nature's typos, offering hope for a future where doctors can fix genetic glitches before they cause problems.

47. **Foldable Phones and Screens: The Bendy Tech** - Foldable phones and screens can bend without breaking, turning a tablet into a phone and back again. It's like having electronic origami in your pocket, proving that the future of gadgets isn't just about being smarter, but also more flexible and fun.

48. **Cybersecurity: The Digital Guardians -** Cybersecurity protects our online lives from hackers and thieves, like having invisible guardians that watch over our digital treasures. It's the shield that keeps our secrets safe and our online adventures secure, making sure the only ones peeking at our data are the ones we say "okay" to.

49. **The Deep Sea Internet: Connecting the Ocean Depths** - Scientists are working on ways to extend the internet into the deep sea, allowing us to explore and monitor the ocean in real-time. It's like casting a giant net of Wi-Fi across the sea, turning the mysterious deep into a place we can visit from our screens, discovering hidden wonders without getting wet.

50. **The Internet of Toys: Playtime, Upgraded** - The Internet of Toys connects traditional playthings to the internet, making them interactive and smart. Imagine your teddy bear learning your name or a toy car navigating a map you design on a tablet. It's a way to blend the magic of imagination with

the wonders of technology, making playtime an adventure in both the real and digital worlds.

Chapter 6
ENGINEERING MARVELS

1. **The Great Wall of China: A Monumental Stretch**
    - The Great Wall of China, with its total length of
    over 13,000 miles, is a marvel of ancient defensive
    architecture. Stretching across northern China, it
    was built to protect Chinese states and empires
    against various nomadic groups. Its construction
    spanned centuries, showcasing the immense effort
    and resources invested by several dynasties.

2. **The International Space Station: The House in
    the Sky** - The International Space Station (ISS)
    is like a science lab that floats above Earth,
    where astronauts live and work while zooming
    around the planet at 17,500 miles per hour. It's
    like having a super-speed treehouse in space.

3. **The Pyramids of Egypt: The Ancient Wonders** -
The Pyramids of Egypt were built without modern
machinery, which is like stacking over 2 million
giant stone Lego blocks with just your hands
and some really old tools. They're the original
megastructures, showing off ancient engineering
skills.

4. **The Panama Canal: The Shortcut Maker** - The
Panama Canal is like a water elevator for ships,
saving them a 12,000-mile detour by cutting
through a country. It's like nature's shortcut,
made better with some clever engineering.

5. **The Golden Gate Bridge: The Iconic Red Span**
- The Golden Gate Bridge is so famous for its
striking red color and grandeur, it's like the movie
star of bridges, always ready for its close-up
against the San Francisco fog.

6. **The Hoover Dam: The Mighty Water Blocker** -
The Hoover Dam is like a giant plug that holds
back the Colorado River, creating Lake Mead,
the largest reservoir in the U.S. It's like saying,
"Stop right there, water!" and the water actually

listens.

7. **The Burj Khalifa: Touching the Sky** - The Burj Khalifa in Dubai stands as the tallest building in the world, reaching a height of 2,722 feet. If you dropped a coin from the top, air resistance would slow its fall, making the coin's descent to the ground take longer than if it were in a vacuum. This iconic skyscraper represents the pinnacle of architectural and engineering advancements.

8. **The Internet: The Invisible Web of Data** - The Internet is like a giant spiderweb connecting the whole world, but instead of spiders and flies, it's full of videos, pictures, and endless information. It's the one web where getting caught is actually a lot of fun!

9. **The Channel Tunnel: The Underwater Handshake** - The Channel Tunnel between the UK and France is like a secret handshake under the sea, allowing trains to zip back and forth as if countries are passing notes in class.

10. **The Hubble Space Telescope: The Universe Peeker** - The Hubble Space Telescope is like a giant eye in space that can see galaxies far, far away. It's like having a superhero's telescope that can peek at the universe's secrets.

11. **Wind Turbines: The Wind Whisperers** - Wind turbines are like giant fans that do the opposite: instead of blowing air, they catch the wind to make electricity. It's like they're whispering to the wind, "Hey, can you charge my phone?"

12. **The Large Hadron Collider: The Particle Smasher** - The Large Hadron Collider is a giant underground ring where scientists smash tiny particles together to discover what the universe is made of. It's like the ultimate arcade game for scientists, where the high score could reveal the secrets of the cosmos.

13. **The Roman Aqueducts: The Ancient Waterways** - Roman aqueducts were like the water slides of ancient Rome, bringing fresh water to cities without using any pumps, just gravity. It's like they built a water park, but for drinking water.

14. **Solar Farms: The Sun Catchers** - Solar farms catch sunlight and turn it into electricity, which is like laying out a giant picnic blanket that soaks up the sun to power your favorite gadgets.

15. **The Akashi Kaikyo Bridge: The Longest Leap** - The Akashi Kaikyo Bridge in Japan is so long, it's like jumping from one city to another over the sea. It holds the record for the world's longest central span of any suspension bridge, making it a leap of engineering marvel.

16. **3D Printed Houses: The Future of Building** - 3D printed houses are created by giant printers that layer material to build a house from the ground up. It's like your home printer got a major upgrade and decided to print out a whole house!

17. **The Maglev Train: The Floating Speedster** - Maglev trains float above the tracks using magnets, which means no wheels, no noise, and super-fast speeds. It's like having a magic carpet, but for the 21st century.

18. **The Artificial Islands of Dubai: The Sand Sculptures** - Dubai's artificial islands are like giant sandcastles in the sea, except these castles have skyscrapers and luxury homes on them. It's like playing in the world's biggest sandbox.

19. **The Mars Rovers: The Red Planet Explorers** - Mars rovers are like remote-controlled cars, but instead of racing down the street, they're taking selfies and doing science on Mars. They're the ultimate space adventurers, without any astronauts having to leave Earth.

20. **The Tesla Coil: The Electric Light Show** - The Tesla Coil can create huge bolts of lightning on demand, which is like having Thor's hammer in a lab. It's the original, earthbound thunderstorm, minus the rain.

21. **The Qinghai-Tibet Railway: The Sky-High Train** - This train is like a mountain goat on tracks, climbing higher than any other in the world. It's as if it's reaching up to give the sky a high-five!

22.   **The Venice Flood Barrier System: The City's Water Shield** - Venice has giant barriers that can rise up and block the sea to stop the city from flooding. It's like having superhero shields that pop up to protect the city's boots from getting wet.

23.   **The Palm Islands, Dubai: The Ocean's Palm Trees** - These man-made islands are shaped like giant palm trees and can be seen from space. It's as if the ocean decided to grow its own tropical islands, with a little help from some very busy humans.

24.   **The Smart Grid: Electricity's Brain** - The Smart Grid is like the internet for electricity, making sure power goes where it's needed without wasting any. It's like having a super-smart traffic cop directing cars, but for electricity.

25.   **The Sydney Opera House: The Sails on the Shore** - This building looks like it's setting sail right in the middle of Sydney, Australia. It's as if a bunch of giant white sails decided to stop by the harbor and put on an opera show.

26. **The Gotthard Base Tunnel: The Mountain's Shortcut** - This tunnel is like a giant wormhole through the mountains, making it the longest railway tunnel in the world. It's as if the mountain opened up and said, "Sure, you can take a shortcut through my belly."

27. **The Falkirk Wheel: The Boat Ferris Wheel** - In Scotland, there's a giant wheel that lifts boats from one canal to another. It's like the boats are going to an amusement park and riding the Ferris wheel, but they're just trying to get from point A to point B.

28. **The Millau Viaduct: The Cloud-Kissing Bridge** - This bridge in France is so tall, it's like walking on a road held up by giant's hands, reaching up to high-five the clouds.

29. **The World Wide Web: The Digital Spiderweb** - The Web connects computers all over the planet, making it easier to find information and cat videos. It's like a giant digital spiderweb, but instead of catching flies, it catches all the knowledge (and some silly stuff too).

30. **The Kansai International Airport: The Island Airport** - Built on an artificial island in Japan, this airport is like a floating spaceship port. It's as if the ocean said, "Sure, you can park your planes here."

31. **The ITER Fusion Reactor: The Sun's Little Brother** - Scientists are building a machine in France that tries to replicate how the sun makes energy. It's like they're making a mini-sun on Earth, but without the risk of getting sunburned.

32. **The Svalbard Global Seed Vault: The Doomsday Seed Bank** - Buried deep in the Arctic, this vault keeps seeds safe for the future. It's like a savings account for plants, making sure we can regrow the world's gardens, just in case.

33. **The Shanghai Maglev: The Floating Train** - This train in China floats above the tracks using magnets and goes super fast. It's like riding on a magic carpet, but it's a train, and it's real!

34. **The Large Binocular Telescope: The Giant's Binoculars** - This telescope is so big, it's like using binoculars the size of a house to spy on stars and galaxies. It's as if the universe is putting on a show, and we've got front-row seats.

35. **The Three Gorges Dam: The River Tamer** - This massive dam in China controls floods, generates power, and helps ships travel. It's like putting a giant plug in the river and then deciding when to let the water flow.

36. **The London Eye: The Giant's Bicycle Wheel** - This huge Ferris wheel on the Thames River gives you a bird's-eye view of London. It's as if a giant dropped his bicycle by the river, and people decided it looked like a fun ride.

37. **The Tokyo Skytree: The Sky-Poking Tower** - This tower in Japan is so tall, it's like a giant pencil trying to poke holes in the sky. It's perfect for getting a good look at how crowded Tokyo really is.

38. **The Curiosity Rover: The Martian Explorer -** This robot is like a remote-controlled car that we sent to Mars to take pictures and do experiments. It's exploring Mars, looking for signs of water and snapping selfies with Martian rocks.

39. **The Human Genome Project: Nature's Blueprint** - Scientists mapped all the genes in the human body, which is like finding the instruction manual for building a person. It's as if we finally found the recipe book for making humans.

40. **The Eiffel Tower: The Iron Lady** - Built for a World Fair, the Eiffel Tower was almost torn down but became one of the most famous landmarks. It's like building a giant Lego tower and then deciding it's too cool to take apart.

41. **The Hyperloop:** A high-speed, pod-based transport system aiming to outpace airplanes through low-pressure tubes. Still experimental, it promises a revolutionary leap in travel efficiency.

42. **The Plastic-Eating Enzymes: Nature's Clean-Up Crew** - Scientists discovered enzymes that can break down plastic. It's like having tiny superheroes that eat plastic for breakfast, helping clean up our mess.

43. **The Crossrail Project: London's Underground Express** - This new train line is being built under London to make traveling across the city faster. It's like digging a secret tunnel under your school so you can get from class to class without being late.

44. **The Tesla Powerwall: The Home Battery** - This battery stores electricity for homes, making it possible to use solar power even at night. It's like having a giant energy snack drawer for your house.

45. **The Burj Al Arab: The Sailboat Hotel** - In Dubai, there's a hotel shaped like a sailboat's sail. It's so fancy, it's like sleeping in a luxury yacht that doesn't rock.

46. **The Oresund Bridge: The Bridge-Tunnel Combo** - This bridge between Denmark and Sweden turns into a tunnel. It's like playing hide and seek with the cars: "Now you see me, now you don't!"

47. **The Adaptive Eyeglasses: The Self-Adjusting Glasses** - These glasses can change focus for you, so you always see clearly.

48. **The Zaha Hadid Buildings: The Future Shapes** - Zaha Hadid designed buildings that look like they're from the future. It's like she was an architect using a time machine as her sketchbook.

49. **The Vertical Farms: The Upward Gardens** - Farms that grow up instead of out can fit in cities, giving new meaning to "urban jungle."

50. **Solar Roadways:** pave streets with energy-producing panels, lighting up markings and melting snow. They turn drives into solar power generation, merging green energy with smart infrastructure for sustainability.

Chapter 7

THE DIGITAL WORLD: COMPUTER SCIENCE

1.   **Coding: Telling Computers What to Do -** Coding is like writing a recipe that tells computers how to make your favorite game or app. It's like you're the boss of the computer, giving it step-by-step instructions on how to not burn the digital cookies.

2.   **The Internet: The World's Chatterbox -** The internet connects computers all over the globe, making it the biggest gossip network where devices share information, videos, and more. It's like the entire planet is passing notes in class.

3.   **Pixels: The Tiny Dots of Color -** Every picture on your screen is made of tiny dots

called pixels. If you think about it, your favorite cartoon character is just a bunch of colorful squares hanging out together.

4. **Binary Code: The Computer's Language** - Computers use binary code, a language of 'ls' and 'Os', to understand what we tell them. It's as if computers are so minimalistic, they only like two numbers!

5. **Algorithms: The Problem-Solving Formulas** - Algorithms are step-by-step instructions for solving problems or making decisions. It's like having a treasure map where "X" marks the spot, but for finding answers.

6. **Artificial Intelligence: The Smartypants Machines** - AI makes computers and robots think and learn like humans. Imagine your robot vacuum getting smarter every day until it starts telling you jokes!

7. **Data Storage: The Digital Memory Box**
    - Computers store information in a digital
    memory box, keeping everything from your
    holiday photos to your secret diary entries
    safe. It's like a treasure chest that never
    gets full.

8. **The Cloud: The Invisible Backpack** - The
    cloud lets you store and access your files
    from anywhere, like an invisible backpack that
    follows you around and never gets heavy.

9. **Cybersecurity: The Digital Knights** -
    Cybersecurity protects our information from
    hackers, like knights guarding a castle. They
    fight off the internet dragons trying to steal
    the treasure of data.

10. **Social Media: The Digital Playground** -
    Social media sites are where people share
    pictures, stories, and chat, turning the
    internet into a giant digital playground. Just
    remember, no running with scissors!

11. **Video Games: The Interactive Adventures**
- Video games are like interactive stories
where you're the hero, the villain, or even the
sidekick. You get to explore, solve puzzles, and
sometimes save the world, all without leaving
your couch.

12. **Search Engines: The Internet's Librarians** -
Search engines help you find anything on the
internet. It's like having a librarian who can
instantly bring you any book, video, or piece
of information you want.

13. **Wi-Fi: The Invisible Internet Leash** - Wi-
Fi connects us to the internet without any
wires, like an invisible leash that gives you
the freedom to roam around with your device,
as long as you don't stray too far from the
Wi-Fi "water bowl."

14. **Virtual Reality: The Other Dimension
Goggles** - Virtual reality (VR) headsets
transport you to other worlds, making you
feel like you're somewhere else entirely.
It's like stepping into a magical wardrobe

that takes you to Narnia, but instead of a wardrobe, it's goggles.

15. **Computer Bugs: The Digital Gremlins** - Computer bugs are flaws in programs that cause weird behavior or mistakes. It's as though little digital gremlins are inside your computer, playing pranks on your software.

16. **Emails: The Electronic Postman** - Emails send messages across the world in seconds, like an electronic postman who's had way too much coffee. Imagine sending a letter to your friend in Australia and it arrives before you even finish writing it!

17. **E-commerce: The Online Shopping Spree** - E-commerce lets you buy things on the internet, turning your computer or phone into a shopping mall. It's like having a magic wallet that lets you shop from your sofa.

18. **Computer Hardware: The Brain and Body of Your Computer** - The hardware is the physical part of your computer, like the brain, heart, and muscles that make it work. If your computer was a robot, the hardware would be its skeleton and organs.

19. **Operating Systems: The Computer's Boss** - Operating systems are like the boss of your computer, telling all the different parts what to do so everything runs smoothly. It's like having a tiny, bossy conductor for the orchestra of your apps and programs.

20. **Programming Languages: The Computer's Dialects** - Just like people speak different languages, computers understand commands in various programming languages. It's as if your computer was multilingual, fluent in Python, Java, and HTML, instead of English, Spanish, and Mandarin.

21. **The Mouse: The Computer's Handshake** - The mouse lets you interact with the computer by pointing, clicking, and dragging. It's like giving

your computer a little handshake every time you want to do something together.

22. **Touch Screens: The Magic Windows** - Touch screens let you control your device with a tap or swipe of your fingers, turning your screen into a magic window that responds to your touch. It's as if you're a wizard, and your spells are cast with a flick of your finger.

23. **The Keyboard: The Computer's Piano** - Keyboards are like pianos for typing, where each key makes a letter appear on the screen instead of a musical note. Imagine composing a symphony, but instead of music, you're creating stories, emails, and homework.

24. **Computer Networks: The Digital Spiderwebs** - Networks connect computers together like a spiderweb, allowing them to share information and talk to each other. It's as if all the computers are holding hands across the digital playground.

25. **Encryption: The Secret Code** - Encryption scrambles your information into a secret code when you send it across the internet, making sure only the intended receiver can read it. It's like writing your diary in a secret language that only you and your best friend understand.

26. **The GPS: The Treasure Map in Your Pocket** - GPS systems use satellites to find your location and help you navigate, like having a treasure map in your pocket that guides you to your destination, except instead of "X marks the spot," it's "You have arrived at your destination."

27. **Databases: The Information Storehouses** - Databases store huge amounts of information, like a giant digital library where data librarians keep everything organized. It's like having an enormous toy box where every toy has its own special place.

28. **Flash Drives: The Pocket Libraries** - Flash drives are tiny devices that can store tons of

files, making them like portable libraries you can carry in your pocket. Imagine carrying around a whole library of your favorite books, movies, and games in something as small as a keychain.

29. **Computer Viruses: The Digital Colds** - Computer viruses are bits of code that can harm your computer, like catching a cold but for your computer. It's as if your computer sneezed and needed to go to the doctor.

30. **The Webcam: The Digital Eye** - Webcams let you video chat by sending live pictures over the internet, turning your computer into a digital eye that can see across the world. It's like having a superpower to be in two places at once.

31. **Cloud Computing: The Sky-High Computer** - Cloud computing uses the internet to store and process data, so you can access your files from anywhere. It's as if your computer's brain is floating in the sky!

32. **Machine Learning: The Learning Computers** - Machine learning lets computers learn from data, improving over time. It's like your computer is going to school, but instead of reading textbooks, it's studying patterns and information.

33. **The Router: The Internet's Traffic Cop** - Routers direct internet traffic, making sure information gets where it needs to go. It's like having a traffic cop inside your house, directing where all the data should go so it doesn't end up in a traffic jam.

34. **Blockchain: The Chain of Digital Blocks** - Blockchain is a secure way to record transactions, like a chain where each link is a block of data. It's as if you're building a digital LEGO tower where each piece is safely locked together with the others.

35. **Quantum Computing: The Super Brain Computers** - Quantum computers use the principles of quantum mechanics to process tasks incredibly fast, like having a superhero

brain that can solve problems at super speed.
It's like your computer ate a bunch of brain-
boosting snacks.

36. **Augmented Reality: The World Plus** -
Augmented reality adds digital images to the
real world, making it look like there's more
than meets the eye. It's as if you're wearing
magic glasses that show hidden treasures in
the world around you.

37. **Li-Fi: The Light-Speed Internet** - Li-Fi
uses light to transmit data, making internet
connections faster and more secure. Imagine
if turning on a lightbulb could also turn on
your internet, lighting up your room and your
computer screen at the same time.

38. **The Silicon Chip: The Computer's Heart** -
Silicon chips are tiny pieces of technology
that power everything from computers to
smartphones. It's like the heart of your
device, beating with billions of electronic
pulses every second.

39. **Voice Recognition: The Computer That Listens** - Voice recognition technology lets computers understand what you're saying, so you can talk to them like you would to a friend. It's as if your computer finally learned how to listen after all these years of you typing away.

40. **Haptic Feedback: The Touchy-Feely Tech** - Haptic feedback technology makes devices vibrate or move in response to your actions, giving you a sense of touch. It's like your phone is giving you a little nudge or pat on the back, saying, "I felt that!"

41. **The Internet of Things: The Chatty Gadgets** - The Internet of Things connects everyday objects to the internet, so they can communicate and make your life easier. Imagine your toaster chatting with your fridge about what you'll have for breakfast.

42. **Facial Recognition: The Computer's Memory for Faces** - Facial recognition technology lets computers recognize and remember faces, just

like you recognize your friends. It's as if your
computer or phone could greet you by name,
just like a friend would.

43. **Wearable Technology: The Fashionable
     Gadgets** - Wearable tech includes
     smartwatches and fitness trackers that
     monitor your health and keep you connected.
     It's like wearing a tiny robot assistant on your
     wrist that reminds you to move around and
     tells you when you've got a message.

44. **Driverless Cars: The Autos Without Pilots -**
     Driverless cars use sensors and AI to drive
     themselves, making it seem like the car has
     its own brain. It's like playing with a remote-
     controlled car, but this one's big enough to sit
     in and read a book while it takes you to the
     park.

45. **3D Graphics: The Digital Sculptors** - 3D
     graphics technology creates lifelike images
     and animations on screens, turning flat
     displays into windows to new worlds. It's as
     if your computer is a sculptor, but instead of

clay, it uses pixels to shape dragons, castles, and outer space adventures.

46. **Digital Currency: The Internet's Money** - Digital currencies, like Bitcoin, are like invisible money you can use to buy things online. It's as if you had a magic wallet that could instantly send and receive money from anywhere in the world.

47. **Computer Cooling Systems: The Device's Personal Fans** - Cooling systems keep your computer from getting too hot, like personal fans that make sure your device doesn't break a sweat, even when it's working hard on your latest project or game.

48. **The Deep Web: The Internet's Hidden Layers** - The Deep Web is the part of the internet that isn't easily found by search engines. It's like the secret passages in a castle, hidden away from the main hallways that everyone walks through.

49. **Nanotechnology in Computing: The Tiny Tech Titans** - Nanotechnology in computing uses incredibly small structures to improve devices. It's like having a team of microscopic superheroes inside your computer, making it faster and more powerful.

50. **The Digital Divide: The Internet's Gap** - The digital divide refers to the gap between those who have access to computers and the internet and those who don't. It's like some people have a fast-moving digital highway, while others have a slow-moving dirt road.

Chapter 8
ENVIRONMENTAL SCIENCE AND SUSTAINABILITY

1. **Recycling: The Earth's Diet Plan** - Recycling is like the Earth's way of dieting. Instead of letting trash pile up like unwanted calories, we reuse it, turning old soda bottles into park benches or playgrounds. It's the ultimate makeover for our junk!

2. **Trees: The Planet's Lungs** - Trees are like the Earth's lungs; they breathe in carbon dioxide and exhale oxygen. Without them, the Earth would be gasping for air, and we'd probably have to carry oxygen tanks like scuba divers on land.

3. **Composting: Nature's Recycling Bin** - Composting turns your leftover banana peels and apple cores into rich soil. It's like a magic trick where food scraps transform into treasure for your garden.

4. **Solar Energy: Sun-Powered Fun** - Solar panels soak up the sun's rays and turn them into electricity, kind of like sunbathing but instead of getting a tan, you power your video games and lights. It's the sun's way of playing tag with your gadgets.

5. **Wind Turbines: The Giants That Whisper to the Wind** - Wind turbines are giant towers with spinning blades that catch the wind's breath to make electricity. They're like the tall, quiet kids in class who are really good at whispering secrets to the breeze.

6. **The Water Cycle: Earth's Bathtub Adventure** - The water cycle is the journey water takes from the sky to the land and back again. It's as if water goes on a vacation, evaporating into clouds before parachuting back down as

rain or snow.

7. **Pollution: The Earth's Bad Hair Day -** Pollution is when harmful stuff gets into the air, land, or water, giving the Earth a really bad hair day. It's up to us to help clean up, sort of like using eco-friendly shampoo.

8. **Endangered Species: Nature's VIP List -** Endangered species are animals and plants that are so rare, they're like the VIPs of nature, except instead of getting special treatment, they need our help to avoid disappearing from the party altogether.

9. **The Greenhouse Effect: Earth's Cozy Blanket -** The greenhouse effect is like a blanket around the Earth, keeping it warm. But too much of it, and the Earth gets too hot, like sleeping with a heavy comforter in the summer.

10. **Ocean Acidification: The Seas' Sour Mood** - The ocean gets more acidic when it absorbs too much CO2, making it harder for sea creatures to build their homes. It's like trying to build a sandcastle with vinegar-soaked sand.

11. **Renewable Energy: Nature's Endless Battery** - Renewable energy comes from sources that won't run out, like the sun, wind, and water. It's like having a battery that recharges itself, making sure the Earth's gadgets never power down.

12. **Deforestation: The World's Vanishing Act** - Deforestation is when large areas of forests are cut down, making it the Earth's most disappointing magic trick. Instead of pulling a rabbit out of a hat, it's like making trees disappear without bringing them back.

13. **Sustainable Living: The Earth-Friendly Lifestyle** - Living sustainably means using resources in a way that doesn't run out. It's like making sure there's enough pizza at the

party for everyone to have a slice, even the latecomers.

14. **Carbon Footprint: The Earth's Shoe Size** - Your carbon footprint is how much carbon dioxide your actions produce. It's like measuring the Earth's shoe size, and the goal is to fit into a smaller pair by walking, biking, or carpooling more.

15. **Biodegradable: Nature's Disappearing Act** - Biodegradable materials break down naturally and disappear back into the Earth, like a leaf that turns into compost. It's the best kind of magic trick, where the wrapper from your snack vanishes without polluting.

16. **Ecosystems: Nature's Busy Neighborhoods** - Ecosystems are like neighborhoods where plants, animals, and other organisms live and work together. Imagine a busy beehive or a coral reef city, where everyone has a job to do.

17. **Conservation: Saving Nature's Masterpieces**
- Conservation is all about protecting and preserving nature's art gallery, from majestic forests to vibrant coral reefs. It's like being a superhero for the planet, guarding against the villains of pollution and habitat destruction.

18. **The Three Rs: Reduce, Reuse, Recycle** - The Three Rs are the Earth's mantra for cutting down on waste. It's like cleaning your room by making sure everything is used wisely and nothing valuable ends up in the trash.

19. **Global Warming: The Earth's Fever** - Global warming is like the Earth running a fever because of too much pollution. Just like you rest and drink fluids when you're sick, the Earth needs us to cut down on greenhouse gases to cool down.

20. **Rainforests: The Earth's Adventure Parks** - Rainforests are jam-packed with more animals and plants than anywhere else, making them like nature's theme parks. But instead of roller coasters, there are swinging monkeys and

towering trees.

21. **Urban Gardening: The City's Green Thumb** -
Urban gardening is about growing plants and
veggies in the city, turning concrete jungles
into lush gardens. It's like playing farmville,
but in real life, and the crops are actual
tomatoes and carrots.

22. **Water Conservation: The Earth's Thirst
Quencher** - Saving water helps make sure
there's enough to go around, from drinking
to swimming. It's like being at a party with
a limited amount of punch; you want to make
sure everyone gets a sip.

23. **Microgreens: Tiny Plants, Big Nutrition -**
Microgreens are nature's small but mighty
plants, offering a burst of nutrients and
flavor despite their size. Ready to harvest
just days after sprouting, they enhance meals
from salads to sandwiches. It's like a mini
garden of superfoods, showing that great
benefits often come in small packages.

24. **Biodiversity: Nature's Variety Show** -
Biodiversity is the variety of life on Earth,
making it like a giant, live-action variety show
with an all-star cast of plants, animals, and
fungi. Every species plays a part, even the
ones that aren't in the spotlight.

25. **Zero Waste: The No-Trash Goal** - Aiming for
zero waste is like trying to clean your room
so well that not a single toy is out of place.
It's about rethinking what we use and how we
use it, so nothing ends up in the landfill.

26. **Electric Vehicles: The Silent Zoomers** -
Electric vehicles (EVs) are like cars with ninja
skills; they move super quietly and don't
pollute the air with smoky breath. It's like
driving the future, without waking up the
neighbors.

27. **The Bees' Busy Job: Pollination Powerhouses**
- Bees are like the Earth's tiny farmers,
buzzing from flower to flower, helping plants
grow fruits and seeds. Without them, we'd
have to say goodbye to a lot of our favorite

snacks. They're the original matchmakers of the plant world!

28. **Upcycling: The Art of Fancy Trash** - Upcycling is when you take something old and make it into something new and cool. It's like turning your old, boring jeans into a stylish denim backpack. Trash gets a second chance to be trendy!

29. **The Coral Reefs: The Underwater Cities** - Coral reefs are like bustling cities under the sea, home to thousands of fish and sea creatures. It's where the ocean's residents live, work, and play. Imagine skyscrapers made of coral and streets bustling with fishy commuters.

30. **Rainwater Harvesting: Nature's Savings Account** - Collecting rainwater to use later is like putting water in a savings account for a non-rainy day. It's Mother Nature's way of saying, "Save some for later; you'll thank me when it's hot out!"

31. **Geothermal Energy: The Earth's Inner Fire**
- Geothermal energy comes from the Earth's core, like tapping into the planet's inner fire to heat homes and make electricity. It's like having a dragon living under your house, but instead of breathing fire, it powers your TV and lights.

32. **The Plastic Problem: Earth's Sticky Situation**
- Too much plastic is like having gum stuck on the planet's shoe; it's tough to get off and ends up everywhere. It's a sticky situation that the Earth could really do without.

33. **The Ice Caps: Earth's Cooling Caps** - The polar ice caps are like the Earth's ice packs, keeping the planet cool. As they melt, it's like the Earth's fever is getting worse. Time to turn down the global thermostat!

34. **Animal Conservation: Saving Earth's Coolest Residents** - Protecting endangered animals is like being a superhero for the coolest residents of Earth. From majestic tigers to quirky pangolins, it's about keeping the Earth's

party diverse and lively.

35. Sustainable Farming: The Kind Way to Grow
- Sustainable farming is about growing food in ways that are kind to the Earth, like using less water and not harming the soil. It's like cooking a meal that's delicious and doesn't leave the kitchen a mess.

36. The Tidal Power: Moon-Powered Energy - Tidal power uses the sea's tides, controlled by the moon's pull, to make electricity. It's as if the moon is reaching down to turn on our lights. Talk about a long-distance relationship!

37. The Great Pacific Garbage Patch: Not the Island Vacation You Imagine - This giant collection of floating trash in the Pacific Ocean is like a nightmarish island made of plastic bottles and bags. It's the one island where no one wants to be stranded.

38. **Green Buildings: Nature's Favorite Hangouts** - Green buildings are designed to save energy and water, making them the planet's BFFs. They're like treehouses for adults, but with eco-friendly perks.

39. **Ocean Cleanup Projects: The Sea's Makeover Crew** - Efforts to clean the oceans are like giving the sea a massive makeover, removing trash and making it sparkle again. It's the ultimate clean-up crew, battling the waves of waste.

40. **Seed Bombs: Guerrilla Gardening Grenades** - Seed bombs are little balls of seeds and soil thrown in empty lots to grow plants. It's like being a nature ninja, throwing green grenades that explode into flowers and trees.

41. **The Lifecycle of Products: From Cradle to Grave...to Cradle!** - Thinking about what happens to products from the moment they're made until they're thrown away (and beyond) is like following the life story of your favorite toy. The goal is to make the story less of

a drama and more of a never-ending happy
cycle.

42. **Biofuels: Nature's Brewed Power** - Biofuels
     are made from plants and waste, turning
     them into fuel for cars and trucks. It's like
     brewing a giant pot of plant tea that cars
     love to drink.

43. **The Food Waste Fiasco: Earth's Leftovers**
     - Throwing away good food is like making a
     giant feast and then tossing it in the trash
     while people are still hungry. It's a fiasco we
     can fix by sharing more and wasting less.

44. **Reusable Products: The Gifts That Keep
     on Giving** - Reusable bags, bottles, and
     containers are like gifts that you can open
     over and over again. They're the opposite of
     one-hit wonders; they're the chart-toppers of
     sustainability.

45. **The Urban Heat Island Effect: City's Fever -** Big cities can get hotter than the countryside because of all the buildings and cars, like a fever that needs cooling down. It's as if the city's wearing too many layers on a summer day.

46. **Xeriscaping: The Desert's Garden -** Xeriscaping is about designing gardens that need very little water, making it perfect for dry areas. It's like giving your garden a camel's superpower to go without water.

47. **Eco-Friendly Packaging: The Earth's Preferred Wrapping** - Choosing packaging made from recycled materials or designed to be reused is like picking the Earth's favorite type of wrapping paper. It's the thoughtful way to wrap our goodies.

48. **Water-Saving Technologies: The Drip Detectives** - Innovations that help save water, like drip irrigation and low-flow toilets, are like detectives fixing leaks and solving the mystery of the disappearing water.

49. **The Importance of Bees: Buzzing Heroes**
- Bees not only make honey, but they also pollinate many of the crops we eat. Protecting bees is like saving the world's busiest gardeners, making sure our fruits and veggies grow.

50. **Zero-Carbon Cities: The Clean Air Metropolises** - Cities aiming to produce zero carbon emissions are like futuristic utopias where the air is clean, cars are electric, and buildings are powered by the sun and wind. It's the dream city for clean air adventurers.

Chapter 9

MATHEMATICS IN NATURE

1. **The Fibonacci Sequence: Nature's Number Pattern** - The Fibonacci sequence is a special set of numbers where each number is the sum of the two before it, like 0, 1, 1, 2, 3, 5, 8, and so on. It's nature's favorite math trick, showing up in the pattern of seeds in a sunflower and the spiral of a snail's shell. It's as if flowers and shells are secretly doing math homework!

2. **Fractals: Nature's Infinite Puzzles** - Fractals are patterns that repeat themselves on smaller and smaller scales, forever! You can see them in the branching of trees, the shape of snowflakes, or the coastlines on a map. It's like nature has a favorite puzzle, and it loves to use the same pieces over and over in everything from broccoli to mountains.

3. **Symmetry: The Balanced Beauty** - Symmetry in nature is when one half of something is the mirror image of the other half, like the wings of a butterfly or the petals of a flower. It's as though nature is obsessed with making sure everything has a twin, just like when you try to make your side of the room look exactly like your sibling's.

4. **The Golden Ratio: The Secret of Beauty** - The Golden Ratio is a special number that artists and architects use to make things look just right. You can find it in the spirals of galaxies and the way petals are arranged on a flower. It's as if the universe has a magic ruler that it uses to make everything look extra nice.

5. **Pi (π): The Circle's Mystery Number** - Pi is the number you get when you divide the distance around a circle by the distance across it. It goes on forever without repeating, showing up in places like the orbits of planets and the ripples in a pond. It's the math world's favorite endless mystery, kind of like trying to find the last piece of popcorn at

the bottom of the bowl.

6. **Hexagons: Nature's Favorite Shape** -
    Hexagons are six-sided shapes that fit
    perfectly together, like a honeycomb in a
    beehive or the Giant's Causeway rocks in
    Ireland. It's as if nature has a favorite shape
    for tiling its floor, choosing hexagons for their
    no-waste, snug fit.

7. **The Circle of Life: Nature's Cycle** - The
    cycle of life, death, and rebirth in nature can
    be thought of like a giant circle, connecting
    everything from the smallest ant to the
    tallest tree. It's nature's way of recycling,
    making sure nothing goes to waste, like
    turning last year's fallen leaves into this
    year's soil.

8. **Pascal's Triangle: The Pyramid of Numbers**
    - Pascal's Triangle is a neat arrangement
    of numbers in a pyramid shape where each
    number is the sum of the two directly
    above it. It shows up in surprising places,
    like the way certain flowers grow or in the

arrangement of seeds in a raspberry. It's as if
nature uses this pyramid as a secret blueprint
for building cool stuff.

9. **Prime Numbers: Nature's Indivisible Codes**
- Prime numbers are numbers that can only
be divided by 1 and themselves, like 2, 3, 5,
7, and 11. They play a role in things like the
life cycles of cicadas, which emerge from
the ground every 13 or 17 years—both prime
numbers—to avoid predators. It's like nature's
secret code that helps them stay one step
ahead of the game.

10. **The Parabolic Arcs: Nature's Perfect Throws**
- The path that water squirts from a fountain
or a ball makes when you throw it forms a
parabola, a curve that's everywhere in nature.
It's the universe's favorite way to throw
things, ensuring that what goes up must come
down in a graceful curve, just like the best
slide at the playground.

11. **Tessellations: Nature's Tile Work -**
Tessellations are patterns made of shapes

that fit together perfectly without any gaps, like the scales on a fish or the cells in a honeycomb. It's as if nature has its own set of tiles and loves to decorate floors, animals, and even plants with a no-space-wasted policy.

12. **Spirals: The Swirls of the Universe** - Spirals are curves that wind around a central point, getting bigger and bigger. You can see them in galaxies, hurricanes, and the shells of snails. It's like the universe has a favorite doodle, and it's been drawing it everywhere from the stars to the sand.

13. **Chaos Theory: Nature's Unpredictability** - Chaos theory is about finding order in what seems random, like the pattern of a leaf or the way smoke twirls into the air. It's nature's reminder that even in the messiest desk, there might be a pattern only the universe understands.

14. **The Four Seasons: Earth's Yearly Cycle** - The changing seasons show us a beautiful pattern in time, as the Earth orbits the sun and tilts

on its axis. It's like nature's calendar, marking the passage of time with flowers in spring, sunshine in summer, leaves in fall, and snow in winter.

15. **The Mathematical Brain: Humans as Natural Calculators** - Even our brains love patterns and numbers, helping us recognize faces, navigate spaces, and enjoy music. It's as if inside every one of us, there's a little mathematician trying to solve the puzzle of the world around us.

16. **Counting Stars: The Night Sky's Number Game** - When we look up at the stars, we're actually seeing a dazzling display of nature's math. It's as if the night sky is a giant dot-to-dot puzzle, where each star is waiting for us to connect the dots and reveal the pictures hidden in constellations. It's nature's own sparkling math problem, with solutions that stretch across the universe.

17. **The Snowflake's Design: Nature's Frozen Geometry** - Every snowflake is a tiny piece

of art with a six-sided symmetry, meaning it has six points that create a perfect pattern. It's like each snowflake is nature's way of showing off its skill in ice sculpture, crafting millions of unique designs that are as fleeting as they are beautiful. It's the chilliest art gallery, where no two exhibits are ever the same.

18. **Animal Groupings: Nature's Way of Counting** - Animals often gather in groups that can be counted to understand their behaviors, like the V formations of migrating birds or the complex colonies of ants. It's as if animals are teaching us that there's strength in numbers, whether it's for flying long distances without getting tired or making sure there's enough food for the whole ant family. It's nature's lesson in teamwork, with a side of math.

19. **The Rhythms of Nature: The Earth's Heartbeat** - The repeating patterns of day and night, the tides, and even the seasons are like the Earth's heartbeat, showing us the rhythm of life that beats in time with the universe. It's like the planet has its own

clock, ticking away with each sunrise, sunset, and the moon's journey across the sky. It's nature's way of keeping time, long before watches and calendars.

20. **Geometric Shapes in Nature: The World's Angles and Curves** - From the perfect circles of the moon and sun to the hexagonal columns of basalt in the Giant's Causeway, nature loves to play with shapes. It's as if the Earth is a giant artist, dabbling in circles, squares, and triangles to create landscapes that are as breathtaking as any painting. It's a reminder that geometry isn't just for textbooks; it's etched into the world around us.

21. **The Tesselation of Beehives: Hexagons at Work** - The hexagonal tesselation in beehives is nature's efficient way to build with the least amount of material and no wasted space. It's like bees are tiny architects, knowing that hexagons are the best shape to store honey, raise their young, and keep their home sturdy. It's a sweet example of math in action, proving that bees might just be the smartest mathematicians around.

22. **The Synchronization of Fireflies: Nature's Light Show** - Fireflies synchronize their light patterns in certain parts of the world, creating a stunning natural light show. It's as if they've all agreed on the perfect timing to flash their lights, like spectators doing "the wave" in a stadium. It's nature's way of showing us that even in the insect world, timing is everything.

23. **The Branching of Trees and Rivers: Fractal Patterns** - The way trees branch into smaller and smaller limbs and how rivers fork into smaller streams are examples of fractal patterns in nature. It's like each tree and river is a family tree, with branches that tell the story of its growth or journey across the landscape. It's a reminder that sometimes, to see the beauty of the forest, we need to admire the branches.

24. **The Waves in the Sand: Nature's Ripples** - The patterns of waves left in the sand by the wind or water show us nature's way of doodling. It's as if the beach is a giant sketchpad, and the waves are the brushes,

leaving behind designs that are as temporary as they are beautiful. It's a lesson in impermanence, teaching us to appreciate the art that exists in the moment.

25. **The Circles of Tree Rings: Nature's History Books** - The rings inside a tree trunk tell the story of its life, with each ring representing a year of growth. It's like trees keep their own diaries, written in rings instead of words. By counting them, we can learn how old a tree is, and the thicker and thinner rings tell us about the rainy and dry years it has seen. It's nature's way of recording history, long before humans started writing it down.

26. **The Spiral Galaxies: Cosmic Swirls** - Spiral galaxies, like our Milky Way, are vast islands of stars, all spinning in a grand, swirling dance. They're shaped like giant cosmic pinwheels, proving that even the universe likes to spin around and get a little dizzy. It's as if space itself is showing off its favorite pattern on the grandest scale, inviting all the stars to join in the whirl.

27. **The Migratory Paths of Birds: The Sky's Highways** - Birds follow precise routes across the sky during migration, using the Earth's magnetic fields as their map. It's like they have a built-in GPS that guides them thousands of miles to the same spot every year. Imagine if you could navigate to your friend's house flying, without ever needing to ask for directions!

28. **The Number of Legs on Insects: Nature's Counting Rule** - Almost all insects have six legs, a number that's just right for their busy, scurrying lives. It's as though nature decided that six was the perfect amount for climbing, running, and occasionally making humans jump with surprise. It's the insect world's own special rule, proving that when it comes to legs, more isn't always better.

29. **The Shape of Snowflakes: Winter's Unique Art** - No two snowflakes are exactly alike, each one a tiny, six-sided masterpiece of ice. It's like nature holds its own art show every winter, with billions of crystals that vanish at the touch. It's a reminder that sometimes,

the most beautiful things are the ones we
can't hold onto.

**30.   The Fibonacci in Pinecones: The Spirals
of Seeds** - Pinecones display the Fibonacci
sequence in the way their scales spiral, a
pattern that's as pretty as it is mathematical.
It's as if pinecones are nature's way of
decorating with math, making sure every seed
has a perfect place to call home. It's a lesson
in both aesthetics and efficiency, straight
from the forest floor.

**31.   The Waves on the Beach: The Rhythm of
the Sea** - The waves lapping on the shore
follow rhythmic patterns, influenced by the
moon's gravity. It's like the ocean is breathing
in and out, in a constant dance with the moon.
It's a natural metronome, setting the pace for
the coastal symphony.

32.   Animal Patterns: The Stripes and Spots -
The patterns on animals, from the stripes
of a zebra to the spots of a leopard, are
nature's own barcodes. They're like wearing

a custom outfit designed by the wilderness, where every pattern is a blend of camouflage and fashion. It's nature's way of saying, "Look good and stay safe," all in one.

33. The Geodesic Domes: Nature's Architecture - Geodesic domes, seen in structures like the Epcot Center, mimic the efficiency of natural forms, like the carbon molecules in a diamond. It's as if architects saw the strength and beauty in a diamond's structure and said, "Let's make that big enough to walk around in." It's a blend of nature's design principles with human creativity.

34. The Petal Counts of Flowers: Nature's Preference - Many flowers have petal counts that are Fibonacci numbers, showing nature's preference for this mathematical sequence. It's as if flowers are trying to win a beauty contest judged by mathematicians, ensuring their petal count adds up to nature's favorite numbers.

35. The River Bends: The Flowing Curves -

Rivers meander and create bends in a pattern that can be described by principles of physics and mathematics. It's like rivers enjoy taking the scenic route, bending and turning to explore the landscape. It's nature's way of ensuring rivers don't just rush straight to the sea without enjoying the journey.

36. **The Mountain Ranges: Earth's Jagged Graph** - Mountain ranges rise and fall in peaks and valleys, like a 3D graph charting the Earth's geological history. It's as if the planet is plotting its own ups and downs, with each mountain peak marking a significant event in Earth's life story. It's a rocky record of time itself.

37. **The Patterns of Sand Dunes: The Desert's Waves** - Sand dunes create patterns that resemble waves, formed by the wind's movement over sand. It's like the desert is trying to mimic the ocean, with dunes as its waves. It's a sandy sea where the waves stand still, letting you admire their shape without getting wet.

38. **The Arrangement of Eyes on a Peacock's Feather: The Look of Nature** - The eyes on a peacock's feathers display an intricate pattern that captivates onlookers. It's as if the peacock is wearing a coat of many eyes, each one a masterpiece of natural design. It's nature's way of showing off, with a flair for the dramatic.

39. **The Crystals in Rocks: Nature's Geometry Kit** - Crystals form in rocks with geometric precision, each angle and face a testament to nature's rule-following side. It's like rocks are nature's geometry kits, complete with the perfect shapes and angles. It's a mineralogical math lesson, hidden in the earth.

40. **The Distribution of Stars: The Universe's Scatter Plot** - The stars in the sky are scattered in a way that, from our perspective, forms constellations. It's like the universe created its own dot-to-dot puzzles for us to solve, connecting the dots to find pictures hidden among the stars. It's a cosmic scatter plot, where every star is a point of light waiting to be connected.

41. **The Growth Rings of Coral: Underwater Calendars** - Coral growth rings, much like tree rings, tell the story of the ocean's conditions over time. It's as if corals are keeping diaries, recording underwater weather reports in their structure. It's a submerged chronicle of sea life, written in rings.

42. **The Egg's Shape: Nature's Perfect Container** - The egg's shape is a marvel of engineering, strong enough to protect life inside yet weak enough to allow the new life to emerge. It's like nature designed the perfect container, optimized for safety and hatchability. It's a lesson in packaging from the bird world.

43. **The Spacing of Bird Flocks: The V Formation Efficiency** - Birds fly in a V formation to conserve energy, using aerodynamics to their advantage. It's as if they're drafting behind each other in a feathery bike race, each bird catching the uplift from the one in front. It's teamwork at its finest, powered by the principles of flight.

44. **The Honeybee's Dance: Geometry in Communication** - Honeybees communicate the location of food through a dance, using angles and distance to describe direction and distance. It's like they have their own dance-based GPS, where waggles and turns give directions to the nearest flower buffet. It's a buzz-worthy performance, combining dance and math.

45. **The Shell's Spiral: Logarithmic Growth** - Many shells follow a logarithmic spiral, growing in a pattern that allows for strength and space. It's as if the shell is planning ahead, ensuring there's always room to grow without losing its shape. It's a spiral expansion plan, drafted by the sea's architects.

46. **The Orb Webs of Spiders: The Circular Traps** - Spider webs often form perfect circles with radial lines, a design that's both beautiful and deadly for its prey. It's like spiders are the artists of the insect world, creating intricate designs that are also high-tech traps. It's a lesson in aesthetics meeting function, spun from silk.

47. **The Lattice Structure of Snowflakes: Symmetry in Cold** - Each snowflake's lattice structure is a testament to the symmetry and uniqueness of nature's designs. It's as though winter is nature's time to show off its most delicate art, with each flake a tiny, cold sculpture. It's the sky's way of sending down tiny gifts, each one a frozen marvel.

48. **The Camouflage of Animals: Geometry in Disguise** - The patterns on animals that help them blend into their surroundings are like living, breathing examples of geometry in action. It's as if nature gave them their own set of geometric clothes, perfectly tailored to hide them from predators or prey. It's the wild's version of hide and seek, with stakes much higher than in the backyard.

49. **The Circadian Rhythms: The Body's Clock** - Our bodies follow circadian rhythms, internal clocks that tell us when to sleep and wake, influenced by the cycle of day and night. It's like we all have a tiny clockmaker inside us, winding up our gears to match the sun's schedule. It's nature's way of saying, "Time for

bed," and "Rise and shine," in sync with the world.

50. **The Angle of the Sun: Seasons and Shadows**
- The angle of the sun changes with the seasons, affecting everything from the length of our shadows to the temperature. It's like the sun is playing with a giant celestial dimmer switch, turning up the heat for summer and dialing it down for winter. It's a global light show, choreographed by the Earth's tilt and orbit.

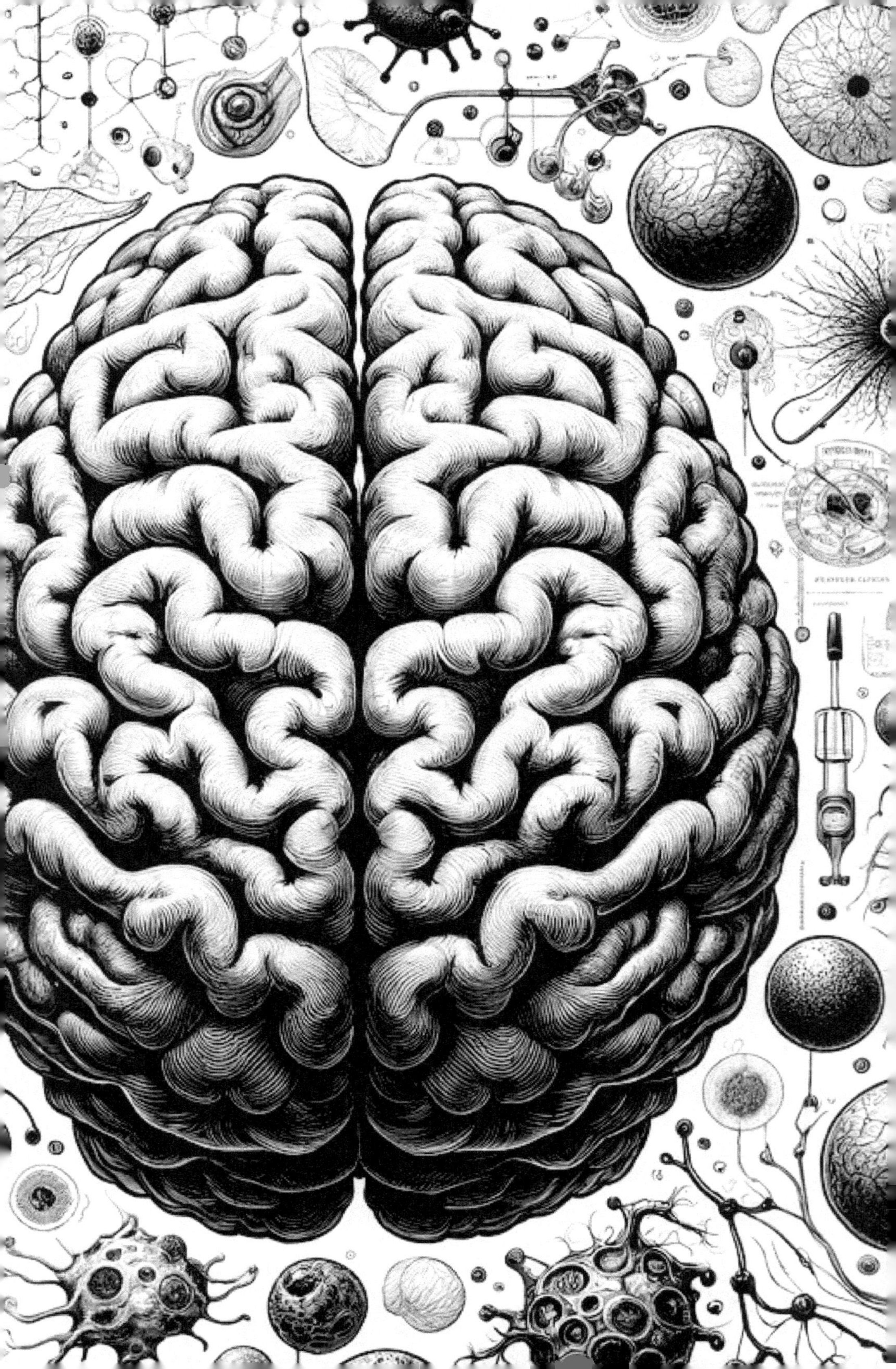

Chapter 10
THE HUMAN BRAIN AND NEUROSCIENCE

1.   **The Brain: The Boss of Your Body** - The brain is like the CEO of your body, making all the big decisions, from when to eat to solving math problems. It's busier than a bee, buzzing with thoughts, dreams, and sometimes, a catchy tune you can't get out of your head.

2.   **Neurons: The Brain's Chatterboxes** - Neurons are tiny cells that talk to each other using electrical signals, like friends texting in a group chat. They're the reason you can smell cookies, feel tickles, and remember the way to your friend's house. It's non-stop gossip in the world of neurons!

3.   **The Cerebrum: The Idea Factory** - The

cerebrum is the part of your brain that's in charge of imagination, thoughts, and planning. It's like a busy idea factory, coming up with plans for building a fort, painting a masterpiece, or plotting a friendly prank on your sibling.

4. **The Cerebellum: The Balance Master -** Tucked under the cerebrum, the cerebellum helps you balance and move smoothly. It's like having an internal gymnastics coach, making sure you don't wobble and fall when you're doing a cartwheel or sprinting to catch the bus.

5. **The Brainstem: The Body's Pilot -** The brainstem controls all the stuff you don't have to think about, like breathing, blinking, and your heart beating. It's like the autopilot mode for your body, keeping you flying straight even when you're snoozing.

6. **The Amygdala: The Emotion Detector -** The amygdala is your emotional radar, helping you feel happy, scared, or annoyed. It's like an

emotional weather station, predicting sunshine or storms inside your head, depending on the day.

7. **The Hippocampus: The Memory Keeper** - The hippocampus is like a memory scrapbook, helping you remember the name of your first pet, your best friend's laugh, and the taste of your favorite ice cream. It's where all your memories are kept safe for you to flip through.

8. **Neuroplasticity: The Brain's Workout Routine** - Neuroplasticity means your brain can change and adapt, learning new things and getting stronger with practice. It's like your brain hitting the gym, lifting weights every time you learn how to spell a new word or master a math problem.

9. **The Corpus Callosum: The Brain's Bridge** - The corpus callosum connects the two halves of your brain, letting them chat and share information. It's like a bridge between two cities, ensuring everyone gets along and

works together nicely.

10. **The Prefrontal Cortex: The Decision Maker** - This part of the brain helps you make choices, like picking chocolate or vanilla, or deciding to study now and play later. It's like having a wise old owl in your head, helping you choose wisely (most of the time).

11. **The Sensory Cortex: The Feeling Genius** - The sensory cortex is the part of the brain that deals with touches, tickles, and itches. It's like having a super-smart secretary who sorts all the feels and sensations coming your way, from the softness of a puppy to the prickliness of a cactus.

12. **The Occipital Lobe: The Movie Projector** - This part of your brain processes everything you see, turning light into images. It's like a mini movie projector in your head, showing you the world in full color and action, even if you're just looking at your cereal bowl.

13. **The Temporal Lobe: The Sound Mixer** - The temporal lobe helps you hear and understand sounds, from music to your mom's voice. It's like having a DJ in your brain, mixing tracks, and making sure you can groove to the beat or follow the conversation.

14. **The Parietal Lobe: The Map Maker** - This brain region helps you understand where your body is in space, so you don't bump into things. It's like having an internal GPS, guiding you through the world without needing to look at a map.

15. **Dreams: The Brain's Nighttime Movies** - Dreams are stories your brain tells you while you're sleeping, from flying like a superhero to exploring candy lands. It's like your brain becomes a movie director every night, deciding to play thrilling, funny, or downright weird films in your head.

16. **The Mirror Neurons: The Copycats** - Mirror neurons help you learn by watching others, like when you learn to dance or shoot hoops.

It's as if part of your brain is playing "monkey see, monkey do," helping you mimic moves until you've got them down pat.

17. **The Fight or Flight Response: The Body's Alarm System** - This is how your brain reacts to danger, deciding in a flash whether to stay and confront the challenge or run away. It's like having a superhero's sense of danger, but instead of fighting villains, it might just be deciding to sprint away from a spider.

18. **The Dopamine Reward System: The Brain's Gold Stars** - Dopamine is a chemical that makes you feel good when you do something rewarding, like finishing your homework or winning a game. It's your brain's way of giving you a gold star or a high-five for a job well done.

19. **The Brain's Language Center: The Chatterbox Area** - Certain parts of your brain work together to help you talk, read, and write. It's like having a chatterbox in your head, one that loves stories, songs, and

the sound of your own voice.

20. **The Autonomic Nervous System: The Behind-the-Scenes Crew** - This system takes care of the things you don't think about, like digesting food and keeping your heart beating. It's the behind-the-scenes crew that makes sure the show (a.k.a. you) goes on smoothly, without any hiccups.

21. **The Synapse: Where Brain Cells Chat** - Synapses are tiny gaps between neurons where messages jump from one cell to another, like whispers passing through the brain's network. It's like the neurons are playing a game of telephone, where the message has to jump from one friend to another to make its way around the brain's playground.

22. **The Pineal Gland: The Sleepy-Time Manager** - This little gland helps regulate your sleep by releasing melatonin when it's dark, telling your body it's bedtime. It's like having a tiny sleep manager in your brain, turning down the

lights and tucking you in, ensuring you get a
good night's rest for tomorrow's adventures.

23. **The Gustatory Cortex: The Flavor Judge**
     - This part of your brain helps you taste
     flavors, from sweet ice cream to sour lemons.
     It's like having a judge on a cooking show
     living in your head, deciding what's delicious
     and what makes you scrunch up your face in
     a "yuck" expression.

24. **The Olfactory Bulb: The Scent Detective**
     - Located in the front of the brain, the
     olfactory bulb is in charge of smelling,
     helping you enjoy the scent of fresh cookies
     or wrinkle your nose at smelly socks. It's the
     brain's scent detective, always on the lookout
     for clues carried in the air.

25. **The Motor Cortex: The Movement Maestro**
     - This part of the brain helps plan and
     control voluntary movements, making sure
     you can dance, jump, and run. It's like having
     a maestro conducting the orchestra of
     your muscles, ensuring every movement is

perfectly timed and graceful (or as graceful
as possible).

26. **The Thalamus: The Brain's Receptionist** –
The thalamus acts like a receptionist for
your brain, taking in sensory information and
deciding where to send it. It's like the brain's
front desk, where every bit of news, from a
cool breeze to a loud noise, checks in before
heading to the right department.

27. **Brain Waves: The Mind's Music** – Your brain
produces waves of electrical activity, like a
personal soundtrack that changes with your
thoughts, feelings, and activities. It's as if
your brain is a radio station, broadcasting
different tunes for focus, relaxation, and
sleep.

28. **The Insula: The Emotional Compass** – Hidden
deep in your brain, the insula helps process
emotions, empathy, and the physical state
of your body. It's like having an emotional
compass inside you, guiding you through
feelings of happiness, sadness, and everything

in between.

29. **The Brain's Plasticity: The Ultimate Learner**
- Your brain's ability to change and adapt, known as plasticity, means you can always learn new things, no matter your age. It's like the brain is made of playdough, constantly reshaping itself with new skills, memories, and ideas.

30. **The Vestibular System: The Balance Wizard**
- Located in your inner ear, this system helps you keep your balance, whether you're standing on one foot or spinning in circles. It's like having a wizard in your ear, casting spells to keep you upright and steady, even when you're trying your fanciest dance moves.

31. **The Brain's Cooling System: The Internal AC** - Your brain has ways to keep cool, like sending extra blood to your face or making you sweat. It's as if your brain has its own air conditioning system, making sure it doesn't overheat when you're running around or solving a particularly tricky math problem.

32. **The Visual Cortex: The Scene Painter** - At the back of your brain, the visual cortex processes all the images your eyes see, turning light into landscapes, faces, and colors. It's like having a master painter in your head, constantly creating beautiful pictures from the light show dancing on your retinas.

33. **The Somatosensory Cortex: The Feeling Map** - This area maps out sensations from all over your body, letting you feel touches, pain, and temperature. It's like having a giant control panel that lights up whenever you stub your toe or feel a warm hug.

34. **Sleep and Dreams: The Nighttime Theater** - During sleep, your brain sorts memories, solves problems, and even plays movies in the form of dreams. It's like your brain runs its own movie theater at night, with free admission to the most bizarre and wonderful shows you can imagine.

35. **The Reward System: The Brain's Treat Jar** - This system releases feel-good chemicals when you do something enjoyable, like eating chocolate or playing video games. It's like your brain has a treat jar, and it gives you a reward every time you do something it likes.

36. **The Blood-Brain Barrier: The Brain's Security Gate** - This protective barrier keeps harmful substances out of the brain while letting nutrients in. It's like having a bouncer at the entrance to your brain, carefully checking who gets in and who has to stay out.

37. **The Broca's Area: The Speech Center** - Located in the frontal lobe, this area is crucial for speech production, helping you turn thoughts into words. It's like having a speechwriter in your brain, crafting everything you want to say into perfect sentences before you speak.

38. **The Wernicke's Area: The Language Decoder** - This region helps you understand spoken and written language. It's like having your

own personal translator in your brain, making sure you understand the story your friend is telling or the book you're reading.

39. **The Brain's Energy Use: The Power Hungry Organ** - Despite its small size, your brain uses about 20% of your body's energy, like a tiny power plant that's always running. It's as if your brain is a little energy monster, constantly munching on glucose snacks to keep thinking, playing, and dreaming.

40. **The Nervous System: The Body's Communication Network** - The nervous system, including your brain, spinal cord, and nerves, sends messages all over your body faster than a speeding text message. It's like the body's internet, keeping all parts of you connected and chatting happily.

41. **The Mirror Effect: Learning by Watching** - Humans can learn new things just by watching others, thanks to special neurons that fire both when you do something and when you see someone else do it. It's as if your brain is

playing a game of "Simon Says," but you learn how to do things instead of getting out.

42. **The Fight, Flight, or Freeze Response: The Brain's Emergency Plan** - This instinctive reaction prepares your body to confront danger, run away, or play dead. It's like having a superhero's sense of danger, but instead of fighting villains, it might just be deciding how to deal with a pop quiz.

43. **The Sense of Smell: The Brain's Scent Archive** - Your sense of smell is directly linked to memory and emotion, more so than any other sense. It's as if your brain keeps a special scrapbook of scents, where a whiff of something can take you back to a moment from your past.

44. **The Brain's Adaptability: The Change Champion** - The human brain can adapt to new situations and learn from experiences, making it incredibly resilient. It's like having a superhero power that lets you bounce back and grow stronger, no matter what life

throws your way.

45. **The Yawn: The Brain's Cool Down** - Yawning might help cool your brain, sort of like opening the hood of a car to let out heat. It's your brain's natural way of chilling out, especially when it's been working hard or when it's time to wake up or wind down.

46. **The Taste Buds: The Flavor Detectives** - Your taste buds work with your brain to detect flavors, from sweet to salty to bitter. It's like having a team of flavor detectives on your tongue, always on the lookout for the next tasty (or not-so-tasty) clue.

47. **The Brain's Healing Power: The Self-Repair Kit** - Your brain has an amazing ability to heal and rewire itself after injuries, thanks to neuroplasticity. It's like having a built-in repair kit, ready to fix up any damage and get everything running smoothly again.

48. **The Brain's Creativity Center: The Imagination Station** – Certain areas of your brain light up with activity when you're being creative, whether you're drawing, inventing, or daydreaming. It's as if there's an imagination station in your head, where all your wildest ideas take off like rockets.

49. **The Brain's Fear Factory: The Scare Central** – The amygdala not only handles emotions but also processes fear, making it the brain's scare central. It's like having a little fear factory in your head, producing scares and sending them down the assembly line whenever you watch a spooky movie or hear a strange noise in the night.

50. **The Brain's Time Machine: The Memory Vault** – Your brain can travel back in time by recalling memories, allowing you to relive moments from your past. It's like having a time machine in your head, one that can take you back to your last birthday party, your first day of school, or that funny thing your friend said yesterday.

Conclusion
THE BRAINIACS WE'VE BECOME!

Well, well, well, look how far we've come, you amazing brainiacs! We've zigzagged through the cosmos, dived into the depths of the ocean, and even time-traveled back to the age of dinosaurs— all without leaving our comfy reading nooks. As we close this chapter (literally) on our super-duper, fantastically fun guide to everything STEM, let's take a moment to marvel at the ground we've covered and the brain-tingling facts we've uncovered.

Remember when we zoomed through space, dodging asteroids and surfing on comet tails? We discovered that space isn't just about black holes gobbling up stars like cosmic vacuum cleaners; it's also about the incredible teamwork between planets, stars, and galaxies that makes the universe the ultimate dance party.

And oh, the magical world of biology, where we

learned that being you is thanks to a zoo of tiny creatures in your belly and a super-cool genetic code that's unique, just like your fingerprint. Who knew that our bodies were such bustling metropolises of life or that plants have their own secret internet made of fungi?

But we didn't stop there. We put on our wizard hats and dived into the bubbling cauldron of chemistry, where baking soda and vinegar aren't just for making volcanoes in science class but are the stars of a chemical reaction party. And let's not forget the engineering feats that showed us how to build everything from skyscrapers that kiss the clouds to bridges that span the horizons.

Technology took us on a magic carpet ride, from smartphones that are like pocket-sized geniuses to video games that are gateways to other dimensions. We peeked behind the curtain to see how technology is the wizard making our modern world more magical every day.

But what about saving the planet, you ask? Environmental science turned us all into planet protectors, teaching us how trees chat about the latest forest gossip and how we can do our part to keep Earth smiling with clean beaches and clear skies.

Physics had us throwing paper airplanes, marveling at the beauty of flight, and understanding the forces that make roller coasters the ultimate thrill ride. And then there was math, the secret language of the universe, turning everything from seashells to galaxies into a numbers game.

Wow, just wow. We've laughed, we've learned, and most importantly, we've discovered that asking questions is the key to unlocking the mysteries of the universe. Every chapter, every fact, and every mind-boggling phenomenon we explored is just the beginning. The real adventure lies in taking what we've learned and asking, "What's next?"

As we bid farewell to this adventure (for now), remember that the world of STEM is always evolving, always expanding, and always ready to blow your mind with new wonders. Today, we're readers and explorers, but who knows what tomorrow holds? Maybe you'll be the one to discover a new planet, invent a robot buddy, or solve one of Earth's biggest puzzles.

So, keep asking questions, keep being curious, and never stop exploring. The universe is a big place, and there's no telling what you might discover next.

Farewell, fellow adventurers, and cheers to the

endless journey of learning and discovery that still
lies ahead!

Copyright Disclaimer:

Explore more at **JourneyJunkieBooks.com**

Did you learn something amazing? We'd love if
you could share your experience with others!
Scan the QR code to leave a testimonial!